MW00777579

Tales of a Wounded Healer

"*Tales of a Wounded Healer* is a dynamic, poetic and instructive book, of interest to mental health clinicians and non-clinicians alike. Many of the life stories, including those of the author, are inspiring and moving. Mariah Fenton Gladis, a truly unique and creative Gestalt psychotherapist, successfully has translated her own personal and professional history into a highly accessible manual for healing and change."

—Paula S. Rosen, MSS, PhD
Counseling and Psychological Services
Swarthmore College

"I was very moved by this personal account from a very gifted healer and therapist. On reading it, I found that my own memories of "exact moments of healing" in her workshops became alive in me again. Her heroic struggles against the misfortunes of her own life serve as a continuing source of inspiration."

—Robert Shapiro, PhD
Professor Emeritus and Senior Research Scientist
Department of Chemistry
New York University

" Reading Mariah's book is like eating my favorite food."

—Dr. Marjory Levitt, psychologist and co-author of
Sibling Revelry

"Mariah's writings are filled with wisdom and clarity. Interspersed through her many fascinating stories are deeply personal insights into the dynamics of healing from traumatic experiences. She is clearly a master at creating what she calls 'exact moments of healing.'"

—Mark Nathanial Mead, Msc
Health Educator & Writer

TALES OF A WOUNDED HEALER

Creating Exact Moments of Healing

Mariah Fenton Gladis, MSS, QCSW

WindWhispers Press

Malvern, Pennsylvania

Published by WindWhispers Press
1434 Treeline Drive, Malvern, PA 19355
www.windwhisperspress.com

Mariah Fenton Gladis
The Pennsylvania Gestalt Center for Psychotherapy and Training
www.gestaltcenter.com

Printed in the United States of America.

1.0

This book is dedicated to Ron, my husband, partner and best friend. With a heart of gold and nerves of steel, your love has given flight to these broken wings and your strength has humbled the impossible.

Acknowledgements

I want to sincerely thank my partners, Dori Middleman and Mark Putnam, both brilliant and compassionate psychiatrists, friends and colleagues. Your love, friendship and dedication to our work are treasures in my life. You are my soul sister and brother. I cherish you. In addition, for over 20 years I have had the privilege of serving on the faculty of Esalen Institute in Big Sur, California. I am most appreciative of the support and enthusiasm for my work that I receive there, in particular from Nancy Lunney-Wheeler, Program Director, whose strong clarity of purpose, warmth and friendship has blessed me with another place to call home, and from Gordon Wheeler, President, who provided the generous Afterword to this book and whose brilliance, humility and friendship continue to grace my life. Special thanks to Bob Falconer, whose healing journey has inspired me to stretch, and whose support has allowed me to finish this book. Much gratitude to Bruce Cornwell, my partner and friend at Esalen for seventeen years, for his gift of theater, empathetic heart and ability to seamlessly intertwine with me on the journey.

For my mother and father, whose losses and sorrows stimulated in me a burning passion for healing. Thanks to Linda Palmarozza, a wonderful writer and friend, who helped get this book underway. To Fetzer Institute for their sincere faith and generous support for this book. To Jax Lowell, who told me from the start I could make it work. And to Ben Bingham, whose enthusiasm and advice have enriched this book. My cousin, Baba Cesarini, who has given me the emotional shelter of a sister for as long as I can remember. And Leona Tucci for her unconditional love and loyalty. To Paula Rosen who has been a long-time guide, a true friend and a keen editor. And Casey Gilmore who gave this book and me a gift of her valuable insights. To Stephen Read who brought his boundless enthusiasm and support to getting this book printed.

The Philadelphia ALS Association and ALS Hope provided assistance and care. To the Pennsylvania Office Of Vocational Rehabilitation and United Disabilities Services, whose assistance has made my productive life possible. And to Bob Barchi, who gave me hope from day one. I feel safer in the world knowing that you're in it. My unending gratitude to my extended family, friends and caregivers for your love, your encouragement, and your graciousness in accommodating ALS into your life.

And for all who shared their story of life and redemption in this book and all my clients with whom I have had the privilege of working, thank you. You have been my teachers, and your lessons are gifts. To Eleanor, whose unremitting love, mothering and green juice have healed me. To Luke and Cole, my sons who became gentlemen before their time. Your magnificence takes my breath away.

Contents

Prologue

My heart broke before the first light of my days. An initiation for a life that would not be easy, yet one that I would never trade. The rhythms, swells and easings of this heart wound have become my compass and my instrument of healing while I travel the under life of things and people. It keeps me riveted with fascination and wonder about why we suffer, what makes people love, how we continue walking when the path is so laden with thorny brush, and how we find our way to join another through the darkness. I listen for the song below the words and dive down to the place beneath so that I may cover myself in the feeling of it all.

My path has been clear from the start. I could have traveled no other. It would take me decades to understand and be grateful for this journey of gathering, communing with and mending broken hearts. It is a way of passion that stretches me to the heights and depths of human touching, merging and standing still and apart, wounded and gazing at one being clearly and with awe. And here I am, breathful and overflowing for as long as I am permitted to stay.

—Mariah Fenton Gladis

Prologue

WHAT'S IMPORTANT?

My life began in an alcohol-saturated womb. I was born blue and with my right foot turned inward. The blue needed warmth—the doctors chose an incubator. My foot needed either a half body cast or a daily massage—my mother, a stranger to touch, chose the cast. Within 2 weeks she was so overwhelmed by motherhood that she called her mother begging for a nanny to deliver my care. It set a theme for my early life. Cold needing warmth and touch.

By the time I was two and a half my parents had divorced and I would spend the remainder of my young life as an only child with a single, depressed, severely alcoholic mother. The stories are horrific, as you can imagine, and too much to tell here. But I can say that while growing up Catholic in the 1950's in an upper middle class area, there was a code of silence that surrounded every family. Whatever happened inside never was told on the outside. I didn't find out until many years after graduation that some of my closest friends from high school had alcoholic parents. We each carried shame and scores of secrets about which we were forbidden to speak. It would have been a "sin" against the family to let an outsider in on what was really happening behind closed doors. The pain stayed inside.

I took on a role as caregiver for my mother very early in life and made a promise to myself that I would never leave home until I found a way to get her sober and off prescription painkillers and sleeping pills. I heard the party lines of "she has to hit bottom," and "you can't hurry the process." If my mother wasn't already at the bottom, then I could never tell you where the bottom was. Yet, she wasn't ready for healing. She had to be pushed. It took me 20 years.

Life with my mother and without a father created a sensitivity and compassion in me for those in pain. Early on, I could see it instantly in a person's eyes; thankfully I cared. Curiosity followed. What was going on? How does this happen to people? How can I

2

help? How can I fix this? There must be a way.

It took me some time to appreciate the road I've traveled. Early childhood has been my teacher. My personal pain could have been my downfall if I hadn't entered its door with determination, compassion of heart and light. It has become my greatest asset; a source of wisdom, strength and resiliency. It has given me the capacity to love more deeply. The choice was always mine. Ignore it and stay on its path, and it would dominate my life. Face it and choose a course of healing, and it would illuminate my life forever.

As I've learned and healed, my interests have expanded to others in similar circumstances who might benefit from my experience. Openly and admittedly I chose my profession in order to heal my family and myself. I don't think this is unusual in the helping professions. My work has been a life's mission; I was initiated and trained for it every day of my early years. And so today, I bless my broken road—the old paths and the new ways—and the trails they've left behind that have led me to who I am today.

Imagine. Look back at the road you have traveled in your life thus far. Is the road smooth, meandering, rugged, straight, straight up, narrow, predictable? Have you been squeezed into it or had room to move? Has it changed? Has the climate been arid, lush, cold or hot? Has it been a lonely road or peopled with loved ones? Have you been safe, protected or violated? When you reached a fork in the road, what did you do? Did you turn away clinging to old routes, or did you venture to select the unknown path? Were you wide-eyed and open-armed when the bends in your road insisted on change? What has mattered most to you? Does your life reflect what's important to you?

You get to travel through this lifetime once. Although the way can unfold, and the terrain can change dramatically, by chance or by choice, to me what matters most is that the road you choose be one where your heart and soul feel a belonging, and the freedom to reach and breathe.

Growth, for all living things, is a natural process of leaning toward light and love. Like a flower caught in the shadow of a rock, it strains upwards to find the sun. The journey often is arduous. When you have walked into enough brick walls along the way, when your inner ache overwhelms you, when your awareness tells you that you can't go on traveling the same destructive path—then your organism quite naturally cries out for healing.

People in psychological pain rarely stand out in a crowd. They are everyday people like you and me who have families and jobs. They also carry a strong sense that something is seriously missing in their lives. They want to be better human beings, capable of creating happier families. They want to love and be loved more effectively. They want to remove the barriers in their lives, and provide more for their loved ones on every level—economically and emotionally. They are looking for ways to contribute, and improve their contact skills in the world. They also want to stop repeating negative patterns, want their fair share of life and love, and want to say something that's been eating them up inside for years. More than anything, they want to feel better about themselves. What they're doing is reaching for health in their lives, searching for a right turn in the road.

I like to consider "exact moments of healing" as right turns in the road; life experiences that offer you a chance to enter into a new dimension of living—something deeper, more complete, more in rhythm with the beat of your heart, and more fulfilling than you've known before. Exact moments of healing are fitting, organic responses to your human quest toward wholeness.

Exact Moments of Healing

We've all had exact moments of healing in our lives. You may not have called them that, but with little effort, I'm sure you can remember transformative experiences, kind words or out of the blue occurrences that deeply affected you. Some of these moments come to you by chance, others you create for yourself with intention. In either case, exact moments are experiences that positively change your life forever. They are moments in time that crystallize in your memory because they are turning points after which you never act or feel the same way again.

A friend was having a long-standing feud with his sister that he wished to correct, but didn't know how. During this time, they became estranged. And then an extraordinary thing happened. Separately, they traveled 2000 miles across the country, to visit the same ancient canyon in a remote part of Arizona. As my friend arrived at the peak of an arduous climb to Indian ruins, there sat his sister. Both were aware enough to realize that this was more than a mere coincidence and, for the first time in many years, they were able to have a meaningful exchange right there and then.

These kinds of spontaneously occurring moments that deeply affect your life are what I consider to be divinely sourced. They can come out of nowhere, and when you least expect them. They can be obvious, as well as subtle. They can be perfect coincidences.

Spontaneous exact moments of healing offer you opportunities to respond: either you grab them, or you miss the moment. You must be awake enough to take advantage of the opportunities they provide for resolution, growth and change.

Creative Participation

Of course, it's wonderful when Fate deals us a kind word, a perfect coincidence, or a lucky insight that delivers an exact moment of healing. But, throughout the past thirty-five years, in my work as a psychotherapist, I have learned that you can't wait around for life-altering moments to happen. You must purposely create powerful, transformative healing moments. When, through personal growth work, one-on-one therapy with a professional or on your own, you interrupt and reverse a pattern of negativity, you help yourself leap to new levels of awareness, broadening your perception of yourself and the world around you.

Exact moments of healing have a beginning, middle and end; they move through us. What is core, and what matches the unmet need, remains and settles in and finds a home in your being. You must be open enough to notice them, and courageous and skilled enough to create them. Then, to fully integrate these moments, you need self-awareness, a purposeful commitment to change, a capacity to receive love, and a soft heart to offer yourself compassion at any moment in time.

I have a strong belief in the contagious effect of individual change: for every one person who transforms his or her life, many more are impacted. The power of one person, in one moment of time, is endless.

Transformations often develop out of a series of exact moments of healing. Some are more dramatic than others, especially when you're ready to confront the deepest, darkest demons of your past. Others are as soft as the wisp of a feather across your consciousness. And age is not a factor in finding these moments. No matter when in your life you reach the point where you can no longer deny the inner hungers, then that is often the moment when Providence gives you an opportunity to re-write history and create exact moments of healing.

So I ask you now, as I ask every client at the beginning of a session, what's important? Go inside your body and feel around for what matters most now. Every body sensation communicates meaning and need. What does your organism need now? Perhaps you have a strain behind your eyes? What is it saying? Is there a knot in your throat? An emptiness in your belly? An ache in your heart? What's in your foreground? What rises to the top of the list? Strip yourself of social niceties. Travel down through your layers of politeness, social engagement, and pressures of the day. Travel down to your inner being, the realm where your organismic wisdom lies, your breath speaks and your authentic self is revealed. Now ask yourself: What's important? What do I need?

Never has there been a time in history when the need for human understanding and forgiveness has been so critical. This is what's important to me. In this era of the emerging global community, our very survival depends on all of us grasping the need to interrupt discrimination and polarization, and equip ourselves with healthy contact skills, and a whole-hearted concern for the well-being of all people. In my work, I see people and families torn apart by trauma, hatred, addiction, and the deep wounds and profound sins of previous generations. I see people despairing that their lives do not reflect their positive intentions to create a loving and stable life. Instead, they are stunted, defined by inner wounds and a lack of emotional abilities and life skills.

I have a front row center seat, to people struggling to find a formula to mend their broken relationships. I see a plague of young women, shamed by their bodies, who are shriveling into anorexia or succumbing to bulimia. I see young men, terrified at their cores, wearing hero masks. I see people, of all ages, colors, sizes and beliefs, aching in their profound aloneness and isolation. I see people every day not saying what they need to say, or doing what they need to do, in order to be fulfilled. Instead, they live by some other rule they neither set up nor understand. I see good people holding on for dear life while imploding with unexpressed pain, often leading to physical illness. I see children and teens who silently, yet passionately, love their parents, pleading to me through frozen eyes to help their families. My heart breaks every time.

In this book, I present true stories, beginning with my own, of people who have changed their lives through this profound work. I describe the seminal moments that shaped their transformations; the moments where they reached a point in their lives when they were ready to face the unfaceable. With professional help, they were willing and able to climb the mountain and shimmy across the big divide to a new road. Hoping that others might be comforted and encouraged, they bravely offered to share their stories. Each story focuses, in detail, on specific moments of healing, and illustrates such themes as the healing power of a loving relationship with the body, recovery from post traumatic stress syndrome, the importance of receptivity in healthy human functioning, the impact of a terminal diagnosis, the need for supportive community, mending of fractured families, creation of self-esteem and empowerment, manifestation of life-fulfilling dreams, development of a compassionate relationship with self and others, and recovery from sexual abuse and trauma.

Although their struggles are varied, they all share a passionate desire to create better lives for themselves, regardless of the emotional intensity of the issues. A determination to survive, forgive and trust empowered these people to face their longing, work through their pain, and discover for themselves a place of self-love, self-acceptance and, the treasure of all treasures, a deep and unconditional love for themselves and all others.

In each story, you may recognize parts of your own story. Let these tales of transformation inspire you to take courage. Dare to peel back the layers. Challenge yourself to take the inward journey in tandem with your external experience, not for a momentary glimpse but for a lifetime. This process of personal evolution is not merely a series of interventions; it is a way of life. It is a way to empower your whole person to master, monitor, accept and enjoy your inner life, as well as your life in the world. You will find an internal compass for maximizing your distinct human potential.

I've designed *Tales Of A Wounded Healer* to help increase your personal awareness, to show you the power of exact moments of healing, to teach you the mechanics of healthy contact and, hopefully, to instill in you the human capacity to bring about change through the vitality of a loving heart. I invite you to consider taking a turn in your road.

The gypsy woman, 50ish, bandana on her head, with hoop earrings and typical gypsy garb, invited me to see something special. She led me into a room with a round table in the middle. On it was a glass box about two feet high, two feet wide and two feet deep. Wide eyed, she motioned with her hands for me to look in the box. I saw figures the size of large chess pieces. They looked humanoid but grotesquely shrunken and malformed. I turned my head away and she said come back—let me show you. She slowly opened the glass lid and reached in and picked up one of the figures that remained rigid and unmoving in her hand. Then she slowly turned it over, showing me what was vivid underneath—a magnificent, multicolored butterfly. The beauty of it took my breath away. She then slowly, gently, put the figure back in its place saying: It isn't time yet. They are not ready.

—Mariah's Dream, October 1979

This dream had a profound effect on me. As I understand dreams, each person, item and relationship is a part of me. So when I first discovered the meaning of this dream, I understood it I terms of my emotional and spiritual development; that I was in incubation, if you will, for a time when I would evolve into a full array of beauty, color and flight. The dream impacted me so deeply, I actually built a presentation around it for 2000 people at an Association of Humanistic Psychology Conference. At that time, I had no inkling that the dream would prove to be prophetic; that I literally would become distorted, misshapen and immobilized. I now take comfort in being the gypsy woman who cares for me and keeps me in a glass box while having sure belief that I will metamorphize into a being of beauty and mobility. I don't know if this transformation will take place on this earth or in another dimension, and I am safe and protected in her care.

—Mariah Fenton Gladis

9

Chapter One

DEATH AS THE GREAT ADVISOR

Life can be reckless. And it can change unpredictably without mercy. One moment you're laughing and carefree and the next you're falling into a scene of horror you never could have imagined. One that screams how fragile life is.

And so it was on July 15th, 1981. In one pain-filled moment in a cold and sterile hospital room in Philadelphia, death extended its hand. In an instant my life shattered. It was that quick and so ominous that the trauma is forever etched in my mind. At 33, I wasn't ready to die. It would take years to graciously shake the hand of what I originally perceived as my enemy.

Back then, my private psychotherapy practice was overflowing, and the Bucks County Institute for Psychotherapy and Training, which I founded, was filled to capacity. Four years out from graduating Bryn Mawr College with a master's degree in social work, I was fascinated with gestalt theory, and I saw the creativity in this method as a springboard to developing my own personal style. By then, I had developed a way of working that incorporated the use of music that was, and still is, revolutionary in the field. Music had always been my refuge from the pain of my childhood and adolescence. I knew the power of music to soothe and inspire the injured soul. I was young, bold, enthusiastic, and always biting off more than I could chew.

The institute was housed in a grand, turn-of-the-century, stone and slate-roofed church near the Delaware River. The church, replete with magnificent stained-glass windows and an aura of redemption, was a perfect location for the weekend workshops and professional training programs. There, students and clients were supported and nurtured by its history of forgiven souls. The church came with a five-bedroom manse that had been in a fire, so the price was low. At 18, I was a licensed realtor, a natural outgrowth of growing up as the daughter of the first woman real estate broker on the Main Line, a collection of affluent towns in suburban

Philadelphia. I knew it was a deal. Friends and colleagues helped me renovate it. It was beautiful. Over time, when playing racquetball, I was having fasciculations, or twitching, in my right thumb. My right hand would cramp tightly and painfully around the racquet handle. I'd have to stop playing and pry my hand off, one finger at a time. The cramping continued to happen more often and in other circumstances. At dinner with friends, I would hide my hands under the table as I painfully pried my fingers away from my fork. However, it never occurred to me that the cramping might be something serious. An old friend, Bob, who was a prominent neurologist, suggested I get it checked out with a colleague of his, which I did.

After a week of outpatient testing, I went in for a thorough workup at the Hospital of the University of Pennsylvania, where Bob was working. He had arranged for the chairman of the neurology department to take my case.

I remember the day, hour, minute, second. I was sitting up in bed in a typical hospital room after receiving a battery of tests, and I was waiting for the results. Still somewhat bright-eyed about the whole thing, I was thinking that the outcome would be uneventful. After all, as far as I knew, I was fit and in perfect health.

Finally, after what seemed like an eternity of waiting, Bob and the chairman of the neurology department came in and sat in front of me. Their mood was somber and they got straight to the point. The chairman told me I had amyotrophic lateral sclerosis, or ALS, a rapidly progressive, invariably fatal, neurological illness that attacks the nerve cells responsible for controlling voluntary muscles. He also told me that ALS had no known cause and no known cure and that I had a ten percent chance of living 2 years. It was horrifying, incomprehensible, and it brought me to my knees in terror. I was so dazed that I didn't even hear the name of the disease. All I heard was that I was going to die. I looked at Bob, searching for something in his eyes that would tell me I would be all right. I saw compassion but also an agreement with the diagnosis. The only hint of reassurance were Bob's parting words, "I hope we're wrong."

Ron, who was asked to stay in the waiting room because we were not married at the time, saw them leave and came into the room.

Speaking in staccato sentences, I was hardly able to catch my breath. I told him I had a neuromuscular disease. My muscles would slowly atrophy and wither away. I was going to die. He put his arms around me and took charge immediately. "Pack your bags, we're leaving," he said. "You're not dying and we have a life to live."

Nothing, and no one, in my life was unchanged by this diagnosis. It felt as if someone had boxed up my whole life, turned it upside down, and shook it until it all fell out. Everything was scattered and rearranged. Feeling like there was no more wind in my sails, I had to reassess everything I believed was safe and sound.

The one thing I was sure of, was that I had finally met a man who I could spend the rest of my life loving. Prior to the diagnosis, Ron and I had been seeing each other for two years, and had talked about a future together. But now, things were different. I told him I was not the same woman he fell in love with. I had a life-threatening illness and that I would understand if he didn't want to continue. Sincerely, I offered him a way out.

He would not hear of it. He was by my side every step of the way, with unyielding optimism and adamance about going ahead with our plans to marry, and have a family. There was no doubt in his mind that together we could manage this nightmare. For many years later, I would piggyback on his faith whenever I could find none.

Three months after the diagnosis, Ron and I went on to marry and start our family. Over the following 2 years we had two wonderful sons, Luke and Cole, who filled our hearts more than either of us had ever imagined. With the threat of the diagnosis hanging over us, we went forward to build our dreams. It was a bittersweet time. I was alive and functioning, and death was ever present.

For the first few years, the damage was limited to my hands. I was able to function normally, and not many people knew I had the disease. Certainly, no one could tell by being in my presence. I chose to reveal my condition only to those who I knew would respond positively, with hope and faith. I avoided all doomsayers, and focused on the demands and joys of my life.

One nagging terror was the thought of losing my speech. One neurologist had seen fasciculations in my tongue, and he noted they were precursors to atrophy. My body had begun its slow deterioration and I was learning to live with that. But how could I prepare to lose my voice? All kinds of terrifying thoughts raced through my mind: people won't want to come to me for therapy; I won't be able to teach; my sons will be embarrassed in front of their friends. It seemed impossible to adjust to that kind of disability.

Slowly, but surely, it happened. At first I would slur my words when I was tired, and my enunciation would become imprecise. I tried to hide it, but eventually I couldn't. I was giving a workshop at Esalen Institute in California every six months, and during one interval, my voice went from clear, to a slight slurring. At that time, I had not been telling my groups that I had ALS. Now, I was scared and wondering who would want to listen to a leader whose voice was impaired? I was afraid of losing their respect and confidence in my ability. Recently, I had been disconnected by more than one telephone operator who surely thought I was inebriated. Waiters had begun bypassing my requests and asking Ron, "What does she want?" as if I were either drunk, deaf or mentally incompetent.

To maintain my credibility, and fend off any doubts, I knew I would have to begin the workshop by publicly announcing that I had ALS, and that my voice had changed since the last time they saw me. I remember it well. It was February 1992.

That was a defining moment in my life. I opened the workshop with, "I am clean and sober, and I have ALS." People were shocked, and visibly moved. Some began crying, and asked what they could do for me. "The best thing you can do for me," I said, "is to let me be here for you, and continue doing the work that I love." They reassured me that the value of my work would not be affected by a speech impediment. Everyone was loving and accepting, and the workshop went on. I felt safe, grateful, and deeply touched by their compassion. That was a distinctly significant moment about possibilities. I was broken and still on solid ground.

I now have a voice-clarifying microphone I use with my clients and at workshops or when giving speeches. It's a miraculous and expensive device that doesn't change my voice but makes it more understandable. When I speak, I sound exactly like me—not robotic—but louder, clearer and easier for a stranger to understand. As an electronic voice enhancer, I call it Eve. Everyone loves that.

Today, after 27 years, ALS has continued its relentless course throughout my entire body. In the early years, my progression was so slow that it was almost imperceptible. In fact, we, and the doctors, questioned whether I had ALS at all. Now, I need help to do just about everything. Fortunately, I'm still able to live a full, productive and exciting life due, in large part, to the incredible support I have from my family, friends and health aides. It is also the people whose lives I've touched in my work, who continue to enrich and inspire me to continue.

However, ALS was a crash course in wisdom. Although career-wise, due to my rapid and early success, I had unknowingly taken on more than I was equipped to handle, it soon became clear that I had considerably more talent than I did wisdom. I needed mature life experiences and to grow old with understanding before my time. Here it was—fasten your seatbelt—ALS, marriage, and children, all in one fell swoop. By my early thirties, lessons of living, loving, and working with a life-threatening disease, set the timber of my life for the next 25 years.

With death as the great advisor, protectively perched on my shoulder and whispering words of wisdom, it is and has been critically important to stay open to the lessons of ALS, and to pass them on to my clients. I now have a much clearer vision of what's important, what really matters, knowing that we can be healthy one minute and dying the next, here one minute and gone the next. Embraced in the awareness of death, I am more able to seize the day, and fully live in the wonder of the moment.

As a psychotherapist, the loss of clarity in my speech forces me to use an economy of words, which I believe complements the work and keeps me out of the client's way. It also gives me the courage to say what needs to be said, often a tender risk. I am more grateful than words can express for my ability to continue this therapeutic work in spite of my impairment, which is normally a retirement accelerator for a psychotherapist. I appreciate the patience of my clients and students. As they actively listen to my words, I assure them, "I have physical limitations AND I am totally present with you in this room."

I also look at life and my work through a very special lens. ALS has humbled me, and forced me to give up the illusions of perfection and control. It has brought home how crucial it is to accept, with compassion, all of who I am, and all of who you are. It

14

has given me a perspective of how it is possible to live a magnificent life, even when infinitely flawed or wounded. I share the lessons with my clients and students about the dichotomy of how fragile we are, and yet how powerful and enduring we can be. I offer myself as living proof that real transformation, and "beating the odds," is always possible and that hope is the engine of change.

From the time of my diagnosis, on the outside chance that the doctors were right, that I only had "2 years to live," I have applied an urgency and an abiding precision to my approach to healing. The pressure has been to effectively and efficiently deliver results to the clients and students who are counting on me. Although I most often believe I will live a long time, I still approach my work with a "hurry up, we don't have forever" attitude. I am acutely aware that every session has to be measurably effective.

Instead of expecting clients to get over their abandonment or poor parenting issues or other major traumas, I am clear that if they could have accepted what happened, and moved on in life, they would have. I also know their organisms will not let them rest. By putting them through the same repetitive patterns, their health and balance seeking organisms will automatically, and continuously, keep them reaching out for resolution, by creating the opportunity to get it right this time. In essence, I keep hearing their organisms say, "Pay attention to me, I need this." With death at my doorstep, I push to get to the heart of the matter and not beat around the bush. I want to know what is really happening here? What does this person need in order to heal? I want to zero in like a laser beam at the central burning need.

I have shifted my focus away from encouraging coping and adjusting; toward hearing and delivering what the client's organism has been constantly seeking. I give clients moments they've always needed; I don't expect them to adapt to their deprivation and trauma. I attend, in new ways, to moments in their lives that never should have happened and moments in their lives that should have happened and didn't. I create experiences that precisely respond to traumas in ways that meet the pressing, central, unmet need, which is lodged in the organism like the eye of a storm. In this way, their entire organism, right down to the cellular level, will never again remember the trauma in the same way.

My Style

The clinical roots of my style of psychotherapy derive from Gestalt psychology and practice. Gestalt therapy, in its truest form, is a lively and holistic, experiential approach to healing and personal growth. It emphasizes the development of awareness—emotional, physical, intellectual and spiritual—and the capacity to make healthy contact with one's self, others, and the environment.

Expanding on the traditional experiential and creative approach of Gestalt, I have designed my own unique style of working. It is saturated with my bias that people heal in an environment of love, forgiveness and compassion. In this sense, I have deviated from the more harsh and confrontational, traditional style of Gestalt that was developed by Fritz Perls in the 1960s. Regardless of his personal and stylistic failings, the basic theory of Gestalt remains brilliant and efficacious, especially when it is heart and soul based.

So as they say, in taking the best and leaving the rest, my approach is experiential, and supports my belief that as people are damaged by experience, so are they healed by experience. To this end, all my clients participate physically, emotionally, intellectually and spiritually in their own healing process. Words are not enough. Imagery is not enough. Human support is not enough. After more than thirty-five years of working with people, I know that when I was offering insight, it was not enough. The organism of each client holds the secret to what it needs, and what is enough. People have to return to the source of the injuries to discover whatever it is that they needed back then; the missing piece. If they need the experience of bonding with a loving mother figure, they will need that all the days of their lives until they get it. The quality of their lives and all their relationships will be adversely affected until they do. This work is powerful, dynamic and almost always profound.

Because we are all unique in our life experiences, and therefore our emotional injuries, the response to a client's need is always specific and individualized. There are a lot of quick fixes that suggest a "one size fits all" cure. Talk shows, radio interviews, and newspaper columns are filled with them. A new approach every week. Prefabricated formulas. No one approach can possibly fit multitudes of people.

16

To this end, when developing an exact moment of healing, I must be willing and able to risk being creative and innovative. I must listen carefully, and help my client access inner wisdom, so that I may accurately assess the burning need. I may need to supply a person with a loving mother, resurrect a deceased spouse, create a judge and jury or create a live choir. Whatever it takes—whatever is needed—I must design it.

With Compassion

Let's talk about compassion. When the word compassion is broken down, com-passion, it means to have passion with, or to feel sympathy with another. When you receive compassion, it moves you out of isolation and into a state of interrelatedness, where you are embraced in the arms of understanding and empathy. Compassion opens you like a love letter; it gives you the safety to risk. Whether with groups or individuals, I work hard to model and establish an environment where people can trust they will be offered support, respect and love, and will be honored in their struggle to heal. Anything less is unacceptable.

In my last workshop at Esalen Institute, there was a woman who appeared hard and rigid and angry. She was in her late forties, blonde, petite, fit and attractively dressed. She was encased in such a hard outer shell that I noticed her disconnection from everyone in the room. She seemed immovable. When she got up to do her individual work, she spoke of the death of her 19-year-old only child, a son. He had died, along with three of his friends, in a car accident on an icy road, where the car had hydroplaned into a brick wall. He had been the driver.

She revealed that she didn't want to live without Matthew; since that tragic day 5 years earlier, she felt dead inside. I could feel a softening of my own reserved response to her toughness, and my heart extending to her. As I looked around the room, I noticed others offering compassion with their tears. I imagined they felt, as I did, there is nothing more unbearable, more intolerable to the soul, than the death of your child.

The work I designed for her exact moment of healing included having her choose someone from the group she could trust, and hold as her son. She said to him all the things she needed to say, including the nearly impossible "Goodbye." Simultaneously, to provide her with perpetual access to his presence and love, I asked her to place an image of her son's eternal love into her heart. Realizing she had been totally isolated and had created a walking death for herself, she began to let the group come close to her, touch her, and offer heartfelt empathy and support. She showed us pictures of her son, and played his voice, saved from a telephone message, while 25 hearts around her broke. By the end of the workshop a smile had returned, the fluidity of her body motion was restored, and her connection with people was realigned. Upon leaving, she told me it was the first time in 5 years that she felt like she didn't have to be dead because Matthew was dead. She was resurrected in the arms and spirit of human compassion.

In this instance, it seems easy to extend compassion, and I suppose it is for me. Where it really gets tricky is when a person in a workshop reveals that he or she has physically or emotionally harmed someone as an aggressor, has abandoned his or her children, or has been a sexual predator. If they are in my group via their own motivation to heal and change, they have every right to the same love and compassion as anyone else in the room.

One workshop had a number of participants who had been sexually abused, and so it was shocking and jarring to them when one man revealed he had sexually abused his sister. It was also confusing to many who had become close to him. He worked on his deep remorse, actively simulating a dialogue with his sister, in which he apologized with such gut-wrenching sincerity, that the truthfulness of his apology could not be in doubt. This was a sacred moment; unanticipated compassion poured forth from the group. One man, who had been violently, and sadistically, sexually abused as a child, was so moved that he could barely speak the words, "I didn't think I could ever sit in the same room with a perpetrator, much less have empathy and forgiveness in my heart. Thank you— I needed to hear those words of apology so much." Extraordinary transformational power resides in the heart of forgiveness. Mercy showers over the forgivers and the forgiven. In that moment, we all heal.

This insistence on loving compassion flies in the face of more traditional Gestalt models that leave space for whatever is to emerge, avoiding direct leadership from the therapist. They are more existential, less interactive, and have no expectations of high-level contact functioning. I don't have the time or tolerance for less. I'm out on a limb here, and open to criticism from the existential purists. I want to set a course that raises the bar high, modeling and insisting on ways of being with one another that are enriching and safe, while consciously stretching our self-imposed boundaries of restraint.

When people work with me, they know they will be expected to rise to their highest selves and give what they can to others. I've been criticized for controlling the group therapy environment by being an active leader, with clear biases. To that I say, yes, that's exactly what I want. I do use evocative music to set a tone. I do open every group by forming a circle with everyone holding hands. I do lead group exercises that build in and promote mutual support. I do interrupt and redirect destructive interactions in a group. I do lecture and teach about the power of love, gratitude and forgiveness. And within this structure, I still follow the organic unfolding of each person's experience.

No Pathology

People often ask me how I do it, listening to people's problems all day long, without getting burned out, drained or disheartened. When I look at someone, I don't see pathology; that is, I don't look for what's wrong with a person. Rather, I see people reaching out for health, looking to grow, attempting to create resolution to the issues in their lives. Even the repetition of ineffective behaviors is an attempt to create resolution. People unconsciously put themselves back in the same old situations and patterns hoping to get it right this time.

My model is not illness-based. It is based on the potential for health and wholeness that we all possess. I assure my clients that I am more enthusiastic and hopeful than ever before, for the human capacity for growth and healing. Fueling this optimism is my freedom to utilize the full breadth of my creativity. And my focus is always directed toward what can and will be achieved, that is, the healthy outcome to a frequently desperate situation. I always have my eye on the prize.

The immediate impact and permanent and profound results of

this work has been staggering. I am awe-struck by how, when given the proper tools and environment, the human spirit can heal itself. The presence of Death has fanned the flames of my passion for healing, clarified my personal and professional priorities and directed my compass when I have felt lost. It has been my teacher, co-therapist and friend. It has propelled me into the arms of those I love. Most of all, the counsel of Death has heightened my awareness of and presence in the here and now, which is all we have for certain.

The past is prologue.

—Shakespeare

Chapter Two

WHAT DO YOU NEED?

A Sanskrit proverb tells us that the musk ox journeys the world searching for the scent that comes from its own hide. And like musk ox, we often search our scientifically bent society, filled with test tubes and technology, for satisfaction outside ourselves. Or, out of unknowingness about what we really need, we turn to drugs, sex, alcohol and destructive relationships. Time and again we discover that personal truth, the kind that moves us to cry or feel joy, emanates from within, from our own hide. We're looking for love, as a famous country song says, in all the wrong places. It is in ourselves, our own organism, our own guts, where we find truth and the capacity to love.

The Wisdom of the Organism

You have within you a reservoir of innate intelligence often referred to as the "wisdom of the organism." This means you have the inherent capacity to know more about yourself, and your needs, than anyone else. For instance, on a physical level, you know when you're thirsty because your mouth becomes dry, and the sensation of thirst dominates your needs. You also know, very naturally, exactly how high to fill the glass to quench that thirst, and get on with your day. That's the wisdom of your organism speaking to you. You simply know what you need. Another person wouldn't know whether to give you a jug of water or an eyedropper full.

A more extreme example of physical self-regulation is provided by your body's response to danger. When your safety is threatened, your autonomic nervous system, that part of the brain that regulates your internal environment to maintain a stable, constant condition, triggers a reaction to the stress: respiration quickens, heart rate increases, muscles tense, and you sweat. Your body is in a state of hyper-arousal and ready for fight, flight or freeze. Again, the body is perfectly designed to know what it needs and to give signals to ensure self-preservation.

Similarly, your organism regulates itself on an emotional level. A vast emotional intelligence continually signals instructions in response to situations ranging from the benign to the traumatic. It does this by sending thoughts, feelings and sensations to help you know what you want and need. For example, if a long-lost friend unexpectedly walks into the room, your organism might register feelings of excitement, affection and a longing for a good hug. In other situations, if an abusive parent walks into the room, your organism may register a need for a quick exit or a need to address unhealed resentments.

In a more traumatic emotional experience such as the death of a loved one, your emotional needs are more complex. You may need to scream to the universe, sob or be angry. You may need to experience despair, denial or aloneness. Others may need the arms of a friend. There are no set rules; you need what you need in the moment. Most importantly, you must know what you need—a level of awareness obtained by too few of us.

Awareness

In my work as a psychotherapist, I guide my clients along a path of self-actualization that is paved with discovery, with many "aha" awarenesses that form the foundation of their transformation. Self-awareness is the ability to turn attention inward and perceive your internal landscape. That means the ability to be conscious of your precise existence on a continual, moment-to-moment basis. That doesn't mean you need to sit around contemplating your navel all day. It does mean you have the ability to know what your navel is doing at any given moment, and when it might become important to be in contact with your body.

As you notice your experience, you may feel your breath. Is it an in-breath or an out-breath? A full or shallow breath? A fast or slow breath? You may also notice temperature, muscle tension or relaxation, pain, numbness and other sensory experiences—such as what you see, hear or touch. Your emergent experience might be a thought, a memory, an emotion, or a spiritual connectedness. In short, awareness is the ability to identify the phenomena of one's existence in any given moment. To illustrate, right now I'm aware of a slight tension in my chest. Now I'm aware of having concerns about whether you the reader will comprehend what I'm trying to communicate. Now I'm aware of taking a deep breath after having said that.

In all cases, self-awareness is critical to getting what you need in your life. In the case of physical needs, such as the awareness of thirst or a threat to your existence, awareness is critical to your survival. Awareness at the emotional level is no less important. A keen self-awareness is critical to living a harmonious and satisfying life in relationship with yourself, others and your environment.

The Awareness and Contact Cycle

Look at the diagram of the *Awareness and Contact Cycle* on the next page. I also call it the Cycle of Organismic Self-Regulation. This is a cycle of healthy self-regulation by your organism as it continually strives to maintain homeostasis or balance. As a step-by-step sequencing of personal phenomena, it has served me as a roadmap for healthy functioning for the past three decades. I am still amazed by its simplicity and brilliance. I have used it, and in fact have changed it, to suit what I believe and how I do my work.

Awareness and Contact Cycle

Cycle of Organismic Self-Regulation

Figure Ⓘ
Foreground
External/Internal

Background

Background

Openness

Post Contact

**Closure
Completion**

Integration

**Satiation
Signal**

Receive

**Energetic
Formation**
Feelings/Sensations

Awareness

Wants/Needs

**Movement
Expression
To Satiation**

Contact

Background

Background

The Figure—Awakening To The Now

The first part of the cycle illustrates the progression from figure/stimulus to energetic formation to want or need—the crucial steps you must take to develop self-awareness.

Initially, I ask a client, "What's important to you right now?" or "What are you aware of right now?" This present moment awareness is called the *figure* and is in the foreground of your awareness while the other elements of your life remain in the background. The figure can be an internal or external stimulus. An internal stimulus might be a thought, an awareness of tightness in your throat, a tension in your jaw or a memory. An external stimulus might be the sight of that same old friend who just walked in the room, a radio turned up too loud or the discomfort you're feeling as you sit in a hardwood chair.

The figure can shift from moment to moment. Probably your figure has changed from the time you started reading this paragraph. You may have felt uncomfortable in your seat and shifted slightly to accommodate the discomfort. Your figure switched from reading this page to adjusting your body, and then back again to reading this page.

Also, the figure can linger or reoccur until you attend to it. If it's a recurring figure, it will call for your attention until it is satisfied. As you will see, every figure precedes a feeling and a want or a need; some are minor such as an itch wanting to be scratched. Some are major, such as the fight you just had with your mother. All call the organism to respond.

Energetic Formation—The Body Responds

In response to each figure/stimulus, your organism moves into an "energetic formation," which means that somewhere in your body you experience sensations or feelings in response to the stimulus. If your jaw has tension, you may feel uncomfortable. If the radio was loud you may feel annoyed. In every case, you always feel something, you never feel nothing. In fact, as Fritz Perls noted, nothingness in itself is a feeling—it's a feeling of "no thingness" or emptiness.

Of course, there are myriad sensations and feelings that you might experience as a response to a figure. Sensations could be hunger, thirst, pain or itch. Feelings might be the primary feelings of mad, sad, glad, scared or sexual arousal or offshoots or combinations of them. For example, giddy might be an offshoot of glad; frustration can be a combination of sad and mad. Every feeling is housed in a bodily sensation. If sad, you may have a heavy heart, tears in your eyes. If angry, you might have a clenched jaw or fist. If you want to know what you're feeling, scan your entire body, limb by limb, organ by organ.

It's amazing to realize that your body shifts in response to every stimulus. If you were transparent like the old plastic Visible Man models, you would see your blood speeding up and slowing down, your heart pounding and relaxing, nerve impulses shooting, and respiration fluctuating. This is an important truth to remember; you respond to each and every stimulus, and that whatever you are exposed to can profoundly impact you from the inside out. Moments can leave an imprint on your being. Some are light and get washed away like writings in the sand whereas others leave a deep mark—sometimes a gash or wound—that could take years to heal. Some leave scars.

Often, when I ask how a new client is feeling, she responds with what she's thinking and not what she's feeling. Initially, it is not an easy question to answer. When George arrived at my office and I asked him how he was feeling, he reported details about his external life, work was good, his family was fine and his daughter was growing up. When I pressed him, the closest he could come to what he was feeling was "blah" and confused about why he wasn't happy. He did not describe any sensation or life from the neck down. He was all thought. He was basically a walking head. I knew that before he could achieve any personal satisfaction or joy, I had to educate him about emotional life and internal experience.

In his work life he was a brilliant scientist; yet he experienced no excitement about his work. He was numb and uncommunicative in his marriage and a distant father. I began with basic exercises in awareness; first teaching him how to breathe, how to fill his diaphragm with air on inhalation and let his belly recede on the exhalation. This took a good deal of time. He was a shallow breather with no awareness of this symptom. After he began to master awareness of his breath and the ability to deepen it and make it fuller, we moved on to bodily sensations. I began with his little toe, encouraging him to be aware of the feeling in his little toes. We moved on to each toe one at a time. Then to the sole of his right foot. Then the left. We moved up to the arches of his feet. The ankles. The heels. The calves. All the way up to the top of his head, and the tips of his fingers. This was literally the first time he had actually focused on feeling his body.

We went on to identify emotions in the body; how he feels in his body when he's angry or sad or excited. I encouraged George to bring his scientific rigor to the discovery process of his internal life. Gradually, he became more aware of his inner self. It was like watching someone awaken from a coma. He gained color in his face and a new aliveness. In his case, it was not so much resistance to awareness and feeling as it was a lack of training. He had come from an intellectual family, one that essentially ignored internal and emotional living. With information and training he expanded and enhanced his entire existence.

So it's important to assess and develop a high level of personal awareness. If you're not in your body, you cannot know what you feel. And if you cannot feel, you'll never be able to identify what you want or need. This will dramatically shrink the quality of your relationships and functioning. Practice awareness, be in the here and now, learn to discern the most minute bodily sensations and feelings.

The Sacredness of Wanting and Needing

Need is the life force of your organism, a vibrant and healthy drive of hunger and longing. You need breath, air, water, shelter, human contact, laughter and tears. Your organism is continually shifting and bringing to the forefront of your awareness (given that you are in touch with your true self) what we call the *next emergent need*. For example, I wake up, my legs want to stretch and I want to be still for a few minutes before I rise. I want to move, reach for my partner with a warm good morning and then retreat to the privacy of my bathroom to complete what is my ritual of beginning my day. Need is presented. Then I satisfy that need and a new need presents itself to be satisfied and so on and so on. Such is the inner pulse of the living organism, always striving for balance. Having a need places us off balance. Satisfying a need returns us to homeostasis.

As infants we start life being totally dependent. Our survival depends upon our needs being met from the outside world. Gradually, we become more able to meet many of our own needs; concomitantly, we become more and more independent in our functioning. As adolescents and young adults, we strive for higher levels of independent functioning. After we have solidified our independence, we must move on to further maturation, growing into a healthy state of interdependence, where we are reliable for others to depend on us and we are able to depend on them. We have matured enough to recognize the value of and need for social and emotional contact, where we are honored, assisted and loved by other people and where we have the wisdom and generosity to allow others to depend on us. A healthy family is one that is aware, responsive and respectful of the ever-changing needs of each family member and of the family as a whole. A healthy society is an inclusive society; one that recognizes the needs of its members and responds in appropriate and generous ways. Needs are both individual and universal.

Now, let's get back to the Cycle of Awareness and Contact. Once you identify an energetic formation (sensation or feeling), you move on to discover what you want or need in response to that feeling.

The truth is that, in response to what you feel, you want or need something all the time. One of the major contributions of Gestalt theory to the field of psychology is this "hunger instinct," which says that it's instinctive to want and to hunger continuously. Freud believed that there were only two basic instincts of man—the sexual drive and the aggressive drive. Fritz Perls added a third, the hunger drive. You hunger not only for physical sustenance, but also for mental, emotional and spiritual nourishment. Many people misunderstand the experience of wanting or longing and consider this "needy," often equating need with something bad or weak. In fact, wanting is a sign of natural, healthy functioning. It's not the fact that you are "too needy" that gets you into trouble; rather, it's how you recognize, respond to and communicate your needs that frequently is the source of the dysfunction.

We have many kinds of basic needs: physical, spiritual, emotional and intellectual, social, functional and economic. Physically, you need air, water, nourishment, shelter, clothing, breath, movement, sex and sleep. Intellectually, you need information, education, skills and fulfilling work. Emotionally, you need bonding, touch, love, self-esteem, security, connectedness and hope. Spiritually, you may need community, self-actualization, a moral path, connection with nature and the Source and a deep reverence for all others. These needs range in their intensity from a mild inclination to a clear preference to a burning passion. The function of these needs is to give you information about how to maintain balance in your life. They are intelligent guides to harmony. It's your job to hear clearly their messages and to heed the wisdom being provided. These needs are your compass to fulfillment and health.

The needs may be small, such as clearing your throat or stretching your neck, taking a walk or scratching an itch. Frequently they involve self-care: washing your face, brushing your teeth. You take care of these small needs all day, every day and their successful completions are the foundation upon which you are freer to address other, more complicated needs. After all, you can't begin to think of what you need in a relationship with your spouse when you have something in your eye.

There is an old saying, "It's not the mountain that defeats the man, it's the grain of sand in his shoe." Neglecting these small needs can make your life chaotic, disorganized and uncomfortable.

How do you recognize a need? Search within your body for clues. A physical need of thirst is recognized by a parched mouth; hunger is recognized by pangs in the stomach. How do you recognize loneliness in your body? For me it's a sensation of emptiness in the area of my chest accompanied by a longing for comfort and connection. Clenched teeth could identify a need for respect, as a reaction to not having it; trembling hands could suggest a need for reassurance. A need for understanding might show itself as a withdrawn numbness; tight shoulders or a pounding heart could signal the need for safety.

You must discern whether the body sensation is expressing a physical or emotional need. For example, tightness in the throat could be simply thirst, or it could signal anger, fear or sadness. If it's thirst, you may want water. If it's an emotion, you may want to share your feelings with your mate.

Needs always are housed in your body, and your body has its own language and way of communicating those needs. You must become fluent in the language of your organism's hungers. As artists are drawn to color, texture, and imaginings, some needs are deeper longings for that which defines us in our uniqueness. They have only to complete their being-ness. A scientist will be drawn to questions, information and exploration, a schoolteacher to information, a carpenter to wood. If you're lucky or well guided you'll be able to recognize these longings early in life. That will set a path of your labor of love that may last a lifetime, serving as a wellspring of fulfillment as you contribute your gifts to the world.

When you do not discover or have the opportunity to follow your path, you can become like a fish out of water. Something in your soul withers. I know a man who was by nature a gifted artist. At the age of 13, his father died. The man had to quit school and go to work to help support the family. He became a pipe fitter and lived a long life of chronic resentment, frustration and addiction. I imagine if he had been encouraged and allowed to follow his nature as an artist he would have been a more self-aligned human being and a myriad of positive possibilities would have emerged. It's tragic when you try to swim on land.

What I'm mostly addressing in this book are the needs that live at the core of each of your levels of functioning: physical, intellectual, emotional and spiritual. They are the ones that clearly express your deepest, authentic needs. They're not band-aids or balms or substitutes. A true need is not ice cream, fame or fortune (although I'll argue when it comes to fine dark chocolate). True needs go right to the heart of the matter. They are "what's important."

These true needs are so important that, in their absence, the quality of your life can be severely limited or impaired. As a dramatic example of this, it is common for infants who are totally deprived of touch to develop mirasmus, a condition that results in failure to thrive, and possibly death. *Mirasmus*, also known as infantile atrophy, is a Greek word meaning "wasting away." In the 19th century, more than half the infants diagnosed with mirasmus, died before they were a year old. It was later discovered that babies who were not touched on a regular basis literally would starve themselves to death.

It's critically important to have a relationship with yourself that includes a healthy respect for your needs and the ability and commitment to provide for them. When you possess this healthy respect, you are more likely to creatively provide for yourself and communicate your needs to someone else in a manner that is not apologetic or implies you are wrong for wanting. You also are less likely to substitute or confuse possessions or substances as objects of your desire, when your true longing may be for a richer emotional and spiritual life.

Confusing/Misreading of Needs

Where you can get into hot water is by confusing superficial longings with deep emotional or spiritual needs, and then proceeding to mismanage them. This can be an unintentional self-deception about what really matters. Do you need that cigarette or do you need love? Do you want that extra slice of pie or do you want connection? Addicts are one of the clearest examples of self-deceivers. Does the alcoholic really long for the sickening oblivion he compulsively marches into time after time, or is there a deeper longing in him that he is too afraid to face or too unskilled or unaware to discern?

One of the surest roads to recovery for someone with addictive behavior is the development of a sound spiritual and emotional life. Often the spiritual and emotional longings of addicts have not been heard or met. When these needs are met, compulsions become easier to manage. When the addict allows himself to feel deep emotional and spiritual longing for connection to himself, others, nature and a God of his understanding, he is on the path toward honoring and fulfilling his true, deeper longings.

Some people can need love, comfort or affection, and yet feel too unworthy to ask for it. Because they feel that needing is wrong or dangerous, they search for a substitute, eating or drinking compulsively to avoid feeling their longing. Healthy people know that their desire for affection is a good and natural longing. They are able to effectively communicate this desire with a loved one, and are more likely to get, as well as give, what they want.

There is an explosion of obesity in this country that constantly points to people's not understanding their nutritional needs. They listen, instead, to advertisers promising satisfaction if they consume products that are nutritionally unsound. They are not aware of the nutritional needs of their bodies. They are physically mismanaging their dietary needs. I have a client who is learning to understand that her constant craving for fast food cheeseburgers is, in fact, a craving for relief from job stress (comfort food). Food has become a comfort in the face of her co-workers' perceived arrogance and attitude. Although it tastes good in the short term, her needs were being mismanaged to the detriment of her physical and emotional health.

Nutritionally, you can feel if your body needs salt or protein or vegetables or salad or fish. Those who are more out of touch might think they need pie or ice cream rather than understand what their body really needs.

After many years of strategizing and experimenting with a nutritional approach to my own healing, I now crave healthy foods such as raw organic vegetable juices. The thought of drinking a Pepsi repulses me because my body has a natural rejection of that which is toxic to my health. This is a complete change for me. In childhood, I used food more often than not to address emotional needs. My mother, obese herself, actually gave me food and sweets to comfort my needs instead of her presence and affection. It took a lot of years of purposeful behavior change for me to identify my true needs; I had cravings, but never recognized them for what they were. My body may have been craving vitamins back then; I thought I wanted a milk shake!

Your History of Wanting and Needing

What does wanting and needing mean to you? Think about your childhood and the lessons you learned about your wants and needs. Were your needs chronically met with or welcomed by an able parent or by teachers who respected your individual needs? Or were your needs met by a tired or angry or unresponsive parent or by a judgmental teacher or priest? Did your parents help you to recognize your own needs for rest, affection, friends and healthy food? If you were overly tired and acting out, did a parent help you understand that you were tired and needed sleep and that you would feel better in the morning, or did the parent criticize you for being obnoxious?

In childhood you also learned about needs from watching the adults around you manage their own wants and needs. You might have watched a parent constantly deny her own needs, while instead, meeting the needs of everyone else around her. Or you may have watched a parent turn to anger and violence because he was impotent to meet his own needs and those of his family.

This is not to say that your every need should have been met. It is more to say that it is unfortunate and sometimes tragic when children learn to turn against themselves, and disrespect their normal hungers, and then substitute unhealthy behaviors in order to deny their true needs. A child may need help doing homework or learning to ride a bike or throwing a football or just some plain old time and affection—all healthy, normal wants and needs. To an overburdened and exhausted single mother, these requests might feel like unwanted intrusive demands and she may rail against them and her child. "How can you ask that of me—can't you see I'm busy? You're selfish. All you care about is yourself." When greeted with this kind of response, a child usually learns that her needs hurt her mother. A template of guilt, self-recrimination and self-loathing is set.

You, as a child, did not have the ability to understand that your needs were legitimate, especially if you were faced with an adult who implied otherwise. You may have learned that your needs were too much or too selfish or just plain wrong and that it was better to deny your organismic instincts.

I had a client who, as a child, believed that if she could get her mother to hold her for just one minute, then all her sadness would go away. She never got that minute. Her mother, who had severe bi-polar disorder, chronically alternated between bouts of debilitating depression and rage. In these states, she was unable to extend her arms to her daughter. My client grew into adulthood feeling unlovable and that her needs were wrong and would never be met. She was compulsively cutting herself, creating chronic crises and chaos in her life and carrying a well of despair.

I needed my father, and my mother trained me to mechanically say to people that I didn't need a father, that my mother was both a mother and a father to me. And I complied. I swallowed that notion to the point of believing it well into young adulthood. As a consequence, I carried the searing pain of loss and longing, abandonment and self-doubt inside, never questioning why. The healthy lesson would have been "Yes, of course you want your father, and I'm so sorry you're growing up without him. Let's figure out some ways that we can help meet your need even though there won't be a perfect solution." That's the concept of creative adjustment. When what you want or need is not possible, you naturally brainstorm viable options that could ameliorate the situation or somehow be responsive to the need.

Did you have a parent who helped you by discussing your needs and helping you sort out which needs were real? As a young child, my son, Cole, sometimes had difficulty sorting out what he truly wanted. When we were shopping for clothes, I would let him try on the red shirt and the blue shirt while he wrestled with the dilemma of which he really wanted. "How do I know, Mom?" he would ask. I told him to try on each shirt, look in the mirror and notice how he felt inside about each one. Did one excite or please him more than the other? I was careful not to pressure him as I gave him early lessons in self-awareness and communication with his body. Often, he would want to know my opinion. I would share it with him, while at the same time, I encouraged him to be curious about his own likes and dislikes. His body would tell him how to recognize if he wanted the blue one more than the red one, even if just a little more. That is a small example of a bigger issue; feeling inside what you truly want, recognizing the signals from inside that express what you actually prefer.

My husband, Ron, grew up in an atmosphere of scarcity. His father had little education and, consequently, a very low paying job. Although he worked hard every day and met the basic needs of his family, there never was money left over for anything beyond the necessities.

Ron remembers the breadbasket occasionally had a package of Tastykakes, small cupcakes that came three in a pack. He knew, that as one of four children, if he took one, someone else would be left out. He was responding to the scarcity in the family and suppressed his need/want/desire for a Tastykake. This was one among many ways he learned to minimize his needs and all but eliminate most of his wants. He didn't feel like he deserved very much, and therefore settled for what he was given, never asking for more.

The good news is that he learned to share and be aware of the needs of others, the bad news is that he learned not to have needs and wants of his own. Even today, he won't take the last piece of pie on a plate, although I often insist that he do so. This issue may be benign, but there may be other more important and detrimental issues he has grown up with that are sourced in that early deprivation awareness.

His childhood could have led him to more of the same in life. Fortunately, he was one of the lucky ones. He realized early that he wanted more in life than his parents had had, and he used the experience of scarcity to catapult himself to a better life, one that included an education, a rewarding career and an endless supply of Tastykakes.

What I want you to hear loud and clear and understand fully is that your needs are organic drives that are good, right and healthy. They serve to promote balance and harmony. Learn to respect your needs and take responsibility for them.

Contact—Awareness into Action

Once you are aware of your feelings and their associated wants and needs, you must move into the second part of the cycle, the contact phase. Whereas the first part of the Awareness and Contact Cycle involves the internal development of awareness, in the contact part of the cycle, you put your awarenesses into actions that provide for the longings of your organism. Contact is the purposeful act of movement and expression with yourself and/or others and/or the environment by which you achieve growth, satisfaction and wholeness.

You make contact through your senses: touching, tasting, smelling, seeing, and listening. Bringing your whole self to the experience of contact involves movement and expression, thinking and feeling, and is always supported by breathing. In contact we may be talking, laughing, reminiscing, dancing, fighting, embracing, competing, establishing limits, taking a stand, giving praise, asking for support.

In other words, the contact phase is on in which you self-actualize, taking hold of the reins of responsibility and grabbing the golden ring on the carousel. It occurs at the boundary where the person meets the environment, where self meets other. As I reach for your hand and look into your eyes, I have crossed the contact boundary between you and me and my experience is somehow changed.

After you have successfully navigated your cycle of awareness and contact, the prize for your work is an organic openness to new sensory stimuli.

Healthy Contact

I believe your capacity to make clear healthy contact with yourself, others and your environment is a barometer that measures your emotional health. I'm therefore constantly working with clients to improve their contact functioning, that is, their ability to bring and give their authentic selves and full capabilities to every interaction.

People who make exquisite contact make you feel seen, engaged and alive. They're the ones who look you in the eye and speak with an intonation in their voice that reflects the intensity and authenticity of their feelings. They are self-revealing, curious and inquisitive about others. They're comfortable in their bodies and fluid in their movement. They make themselves understood and can be counted on for action. They see people in all their distinctiveness and revel at how differences in people make for a fuller world for all.

It is through authentic contact that you cross the invisible boundary between where you end and others begin. When you move out of self-awareness and bring yourself to another, you see that person with your eyes, hear her with your ears. You extend your hand and give your interest and curiosity. You assess what is you and what is they, and where you may overlap. Contact can occur in a moment in which you nod your head or in an hour-long discussion. It is the way in which you are with another. By this interaction you both give to and receive from the experience. You acquire from the environment and give to it. You impact and are impacted by the exchange. By making full and authentic contact, you expand your experience and are changed by your interaction in both subtle and profound ways.

Making healthy contact is not as easy as it sounds. Most of us need to learn contact functioning skills and, as we mature, we to continue to develop them. The ability to fully see a flower in its many shapes and colors, twists and turns is difficult. Imagine how much attention it takes, at any given moment, to fully see another human being, much less respond to that person's needs.

This issue of meeting needs may seem simple to some, but it is the mismanagement of personal needs that so often ruins relationships and entire lives. The divorce rate in the United States is now at 52%, and it is higher in some places. Clearly, people are not getting their needs met. A good marriage counselor will help each partner define his or her needs, and learn to express them in more effective ways.

In a healthy marriage, partners stay in fresh current contact with each other. One partner is effectively wondering and asking, "Who are you now?" on a continual basis, rather than assuming that they're exactly the same as they were the day before. Each asks questions like, "What are you thinking?" "How do you feel about such and such?" "What's important for you today?" Each has interest in the details, evolutions and changing subtleties of the other. We all resist contact and too frequently see what we imagine or want to see rather than what is.

In working with couples, I often see one person resent the very qualities that originally made the other attractive. It is helpful to remind the couple that these qualities are still present. They need to learn to shift their resentments back to appreciating their differences and allow their appreciation to bring excitement back into the relationship.

Contact has been defined by Dick Price, co-founder of Esalen Institute, as the recognition of similarities and the appreciation of differences. I'd like to expand that definition to include interest in and identification with the needs of others. Some people say they want a spouse with whom they have no differences ("We both like blue." "We both voted for Clinton.") This likely will turn out to be a limited way to make contact. Although it is true that a high degree of similarities makes for compatibility and ease in a relationship, differences often add spice, aliveness and an opportunity for growth. A relationship with no differences could prove to be flat and limiting. Eventually, the relationship might be experienced as empty or lifeless. Contact with others from whom you are different offers an opportunity for growth. We all have similarities, and we all have differences.

On a global scale, nations often clash over their demands for sameness. Rather than appreciating cultural differences, and making room for them, they engage in bitter conflict. I encourage you to expand your tolerance for the ways in which people differ from you, to be curious and to find out more about others. Discover what is in your own background that causes such a strong reaction to someone different from you. What is it about the emotional charge that is offending you? That insight may release you from your unyielding prejudices and open the way to experience differences, not as a threat, but as a valuable addition to your life journey.

Healthy contact functioning is perhaps the single most important capacity we possess. It is what makes or breaks relationships, binds or destroys families, and allies or alienates nations. It is what enables you to get your love across. To not have this capacity is to be emotionally and interpersonally disabled. I cannot stress strongly enough how critical it is to expand your capacity to make healthy contact.

Movement and Expression

The beginning of the contact phase of the cycle asks you to respond to your wants and needs by moving out and/or expressing yourself effectively and totally until you feel a sense of completion. If you are thirsty, you may need to move across the room, get a glass of water and drink it. If you are sad, you may need to move and express yourself by picking up the phone, dialing and talking to a friend. For longing, you may need to thoughtfully address a long-standing issue with your husband, wife or friend. For resentment, you may need to skillfully express your anger and hurt toward a boss or parent.

Some of us are more facile with expression than movement. Able expressers seem to easily speak their emotions with words. They move their feelings from the inside out. They are crisp and clear in their communication and can carry on lengthy and lively conversations that include emotional seasoning and accurate information. They can present objective and subjective data clearly and with purpose. In marriage or family life they also are the ones who ask, "How was your day?" "How do you feel about such-and-such?" They are self-aware and self-revealing, that is, transparent in disclosing precisely how they feel.

Then, of course, there are people who are more verbal than physical, yet still lack the communication skills necessary to ensure satisfactory, enjoyable, authentic interaction.

Others respond energetically to a want or need through the use of their bodies. I call them movers. In response to their emotions, they move out on their own behalf. Every feeling has a natural accompanying motion. In fact, the word *emotion* has the word *motion* in it. However, often you see people who appear to have no life force or energy in their bodies. They appear stiff or rigid with non-descript movement. For whatever reason, there is a restriction of their existence on the physical plane. This restriction threatens and often sabotages the satisfaction of their wants and needs.

Movers go, do and build. They are action-oriented taskmasters. They dance. They love touch. Play music. Take out the garbage. Lock the door and turn out the lights. They walk the dog. They're affectionate. They cook. Their bodies are actively involved in communicating and carrying out their feelings, wants and needs.

Likewise there are people who are naturally more physical who, for some reason—shyness or lack of experience or trauma—hold their bodies back when in contact with others. They do not possess a natural ease in the art of touch, especially if they have received toxic touch from a parent or others. The job of going beyond that toxicity and into the experience of positive touch can be a difficult and long process. So, you might have a marathon runner running away from the tender moments of touch.

In a relationship of classic movers and expressers, one partner might be able to make mad, passionate love, but not say, "I love you," whereas the other partner might be able to say, "I love you," morning, noon and night but not be able to be a lively, sexual partner. Typically, the expresser will say something like, "You never talk to me and tell me you love me." The mover will respond with, "Didn't I just spend the whole day fixing your closet?" When an expresser doesn't feel loved by a mover, I often tell them my friend Dolly's expression, "Watch the feet." If your partner's feet are moving in your direction in response to your need, that is an expression of love. Recognize it as such. Ideally, movers and expressers learn from each other and expand their abilities to both move and express in healthy ways. After many years of working with couples, I've noticed how often a mover and an expresser marry and drive each other crazy.

Longing sometimes is a request to yourself for action and labor. I know someone who deeply wants to achieve artistic success, yet resists movement such as applying for the education she needs to advance herself. She won't move out on her own behalf, and instead, remains in a box of confusion, dissatisfaction, unmet longing and an underdeveloped life. You've probably met the type. You want to give her a kick in the butt and say, "Move! Don't just stay where you are." I also had a client who was very bright and desperately longed to find his place in the world. Instead, he kept himself on public assistance, living on a shoestring, was chronically late and isolated. He too wouldn't move. These non-movers are the ultimate frustrators, sabotaging any attempt from the outside to prod them into action. They live with their talent buried alive, never experiencing the excitement and satisfaction of fully exerting who they are, never knowing the sense of pride and accomplishment that derives from matching movement to the intensity of their need.

Think about yourself. Are you more of a mover or an expresser? In your professional and personal life, are your communications skills working for you? Are your words original, expansive and precise? Are you speaking your own language or that of your family of origin? Do you stay aware of your body and bring it fully into your life in positive ways? Do you feel the joy and pleasure of movement? Are you embodied (in your body) when you're with others? Do you move toward that which is healthy and away from that which is toxic? Do you restrict or expand your physical actions? Do you have a full capacity to give and receive affection and sexual fulfillment?

If you have impediments to your expressions or movement, you need to identify them and figure out what needs your attention and/or healing. It's true that you probably need to spend your entire lifetime honing your skills in moving and expressing.

Asking for What You Want

Moving out into the world, expressing your needs, and asking for what you want can be a scary business. It takes strength and assertiveness to ask your boss for a raise; it takes tact and directness to ask your siblings for help with an aging parent. Putting yourself out there and asking for what you want can be fraught with risk. You might hear a no. You might get into an argument. You might be disappointed. On the other hand, your siblings may not have been paying enough attention to the situation and may be glad you asked for help. Your boss may have been distracted and may not have realized it was time to honor you with a raise. Neither might have happened without your movement or expression. The capacity to represent yourself well in the world, and move out on your own behalf, ensures that your needs are communicated, known and respected.

Sometimes, when you want something, you simply need to gracefully ask for it. At a recent Thanksgiving dinner, which is traditionally at our house, my cousin made the announcement that she needed help cleaning the dishes and a load of pots and pans stacked in the sink. Leftovers needed to be put away, and general cleanup was necessary. She was even more specific; she asked the men to help. They had not volunteered, but all got up willingly and participated. She didn't whine, complain, accuse or transfer any negative attitude. She simply and politely asked for what she needed. It makes it easier on the person you are addressing when you are clean and clear in your communication.

Children often respond well to this concept. My friend Ben's young son, Nathan, said to his dad, "Don't ask me if I want to help you with something, just ask me to help!"

Ron tells the story of negotiating a special situation with a caterer with whom we had worked for years. This small problem had the possibility of becoming a deal breaker. Her husband overheard their animated conversation and, knowing our long history, politely interjected the old Indian saying. "Never trip over small stones." To get each of their needs met, they needed to shift away from complaints and judgments to a fairly expressed mutual exchange of requests. They needed to simply and respectfully ask for what each wanted.

Of course you don't want to leave yourself alone out on a limb. When you take the risk to make a request, you want to be there to comfort and support yourself if you hear a "no." For example, if you work up the courage to ask out on a date someone you think is special, and she says no, the last thing you want to say to yourself is, "She was too good for you, anyway. You should never have asked her out." You do want to hear something like, "Good for you, you went for it. She doesn't know what she's missing." Even if the other person does not come through for you, you must be there with compassion and support for yourself.

A common mistake people often make is asking for what they don't want instead of asking for what they do want. They tend to create a battleground instead of a negotiating table. They fight to get their needs met. "Don't leave your room like a pigsty" instead of "Please take the time now to clean up your room. It will help you and me feel better." I overheard a coach say to one of his male players, "Don't kick the ball like a girl" instead of "Make sure you leave enough space between yourself and the ball so that you can make a full kick." A wife might say, "Don't track mud all over this house" instead of "Please leave your work boots at the door." Or "Stop criticizing me" instead of "If you're giving me difficult feedback, please do it with kindness and respect." One is an underlying or outright attack. The other is a positive request.

When people rant about what they don't want instead of openly expressing what they do want, they often assume the other does not want to give them what they want. This is frequently not the case. A spouse often does want to give his mate what she wants but is responding defensively to an attack. Try assuming that your mate really does want to meet your needs and approach her from that perspective. Instead of "Stop driving like a maniac" you might try "Honey, I know our family's safety is important to you. Would you consider driving more slowly?" Often it takes a considerable pause to figure out how to say what you do want in a way that supports the other person as well as yourself. It's well worth the effort.

Another way to productively ask for what you want is by making "I" statements instead of "You" statements. In other words, talk about yourself and your needs, rather than making statements about the other person's behavior or character. Again, this involves openly expressing your needs. Don't bypass being vulnerable by saying, "You don't do this" or "You never do that." Rather, make I statements such as "I need this" or "I need that." Instead of saying, "You never tell me I'm pretty" say "I would really love it if you would tell me you think I'm beautiful." In this way, instead of placing the responsibility and blame outside yourself, you own your own needs and wants and take responsibility for reaching out and getting them met. Needless to say, this makes it way easier for your mate to be generous with you. If you ridicule or belittle, point your finger and say "You," "You," "You," it usually creates defensiveness, and a lack of cooperation or motivation. The lesson here is to turn your criticism into a request.

New clients often resist the idea of revealing their needs and asking for what they want. "If I have to ask for it, it doesn't count. What good is it?" they ask. They want to hold onto the childhood notion that others should instinctively know their needs, read their minds and give them what they want. All of this without any direct communication about what they feel and need. They don't want to do the work of artful negotiation; instead, they long for the other to know them well enough and anticipate their every need. This is a romanticized and idealized view of human interaction. We are each responsible for managing our own needs, and that includes revealing them in skillful and easily heard ways. Ironically, this sometimes is more difficult in our closest relationships, where we are highly vulnerable and have the most at stake.

Being vulnerable and self-revealing generally is not perceived as a strength. But, believe me, it is a courageous act. And it is essential. It is the only way to be deeply known and to have your needs met. Your most intimate relationships require you to be simultaneously bold and fragile when expressing and revealing your innermost emotional needs.

Our deepest emotional needs often are reflective of our deepest pain. Think about your own deepest pain and the need associated with that pain. For me, it's the pain of loss and abandonment; the loss of my father and abandonment by my mother through alcoholism. Those losses created in me a deep need for a partner whom I could trust impeccably and who would protect, cherish and stand by me. I took a long time before I found Ron, with his nerves of steel and heart of gold. When I revealed to him my deep needs borne of my family history, he responded with strength, love and protectiveness. It was a risk, since I didn't know Ron well enough to trust that he would stay, and not run. Although I felt extremely vulnerable, it was not a healthy option for me to be in a relationship with anyone who did not know and love me at the deepest level.

I encourage you to risk being self-revealing and transparent with your closest friends and life partner. If you need reassurance, let him know. If you need her to believe in you and be proud of you, let her know. If you need to be held while you cry, reveal that need. And vice-versa. Inquire about his deeper emotional needs, and do your best to meet them. At workshops, I see time and again that as people reveal their pain and reach out for comfort (even from strangers), barriers to closeness fall away, and bonds begin to develop, some lasting a lifetime. Peeling away the layers that hide your deeper needs is what facilitates close connections.

One small useful tool is to reveal the power that certain words or behaviors have for us. We all have our own set of what I call *magic words,* usually sourced in childhood pain and always associated with our deepest pain. They are the words that can comfort our raw wounds or strike a chord that resonates with our heart and soul. For some it may be "I'll never leave you," "You are precious to me," "I'm so proud of you," "You are a real treasure," "You're going to be all right," "I'll protect you," "You're beautiful." These are the words our marriage partners need to know. They give them access and power to help meet our deepest emotional needs. If your partner agrees to lovingly speak your magic words, the experience can be a powerful one. Think about yourself. What words would soothe your deepest pain? What are the words you have always longed to hear?

There are times when it may be too abrasive to be totally direct and it is more advantageous to set the stage for creating the occasion of having your needs met. Make it as easy as possible for the other. Take positive initiative. Give clues to what you need. Give opportunity. You want to facilitate an ability to know what you need and provide for it. You might do it by a joke or by putting your arms gently around your partner and saying you need to be held. I do this a lot with adult children and parent healing work. If you want your father, for the first time in his life, to tell you he loves you, you want to make it as easy as possible for him to do so. You don't want to criticize him for past inaction or complain that he always lets you down. You want to let him know how much his love means to you, and how he could positively change your life by speaking those words of love now.

At a workshop, a client shared that his mother was on her deathbed. She had been violently abusive to him as a child. I encouraged him to take the chance to go to her and tell her how important it was for him to hear the words, "I love you, son," before she died. So he could experience the possibility of it happening, I had him practice expressing his need and pain to a person playing the part of his mother so that he could experience the possibility of it happening. I made sure he understood that it was more important that he had the courage to reveal his deepest needs than it was that they be met. He knew he would be all right if she were not able to respond.

At the hospital, he was able to ask her to say, "I love you." He went one step further and inquired, uncritically, why she had beaten him so often. Because of his positive and non-judgmental approach, she was able to explain that that she was repeating her own experiences as a child and that this was the only way she knew how to be a parent. She apologized and told him she loved him very much and was so sorry for the pain she had caused. He had had to break through years of his own bitterness and unforgiveness to set the stage for this tender moment finally to occur.

Of course, this doesn't mean you will or should get everything you want. It does mean you need to respect and empathize with your own personal longings as well as make a creative adjustment when you can't have what you want. For instance, if you're longing for a love relationship and you don't have one at the moment, you'll need to say to yourself, "I hear how much you're wanting a partner right now and I can't provide that just yet. Let me assure you I'm with you and I treasure you and will do everything I can to prepare you to be ready for that right person when he or she comes along." Remember, when it comes to needing love, you cannot expect more from someone else than you are able to give to yourself. I frequently tell my students, "arrive already loved."

Receptivity

Receiving is an activity. Often this is news to people. They've never understood, nor even contemplated the nature of receptivity. When they are presented with a gift, it is as if all activity stops; they go into passive mode. In truth, an essential activity has just begun. Real receiving necessitates being in full, clear contact with yourself, your body and the other person. It is a purposeful action that is fueled by concentration and awareness of self and other, and it is grounded in the intention to receive well. It requires grateful absorbing of the gift, whether it's a smile, an expression of love, a physical presence, a sexual union, a massage, a touch, a piece of art, an orchid, a complement, a favor, an apology. The list is endless; from the ever so subtle to the magnificence of nature and the grandeur of true love. The simple truth is the less you receive, the less fulfillment you'll experience in life. So when you have learned to move out in the world in response to your needs and to express them with skill and authenticity, it will all be for naught if you don't have the ability to fully receive from yourself and others.

Receiving is not about what you get or how much you accumulate in life or about grasping. There are countless wealthy people who are at a loss as to why they are so unhappy. They mistake external wealth with internal prosperity. There are others who demand love or respect or power and get it. But, because of the forced nature of the giving, they don't get what they really want. Receiving is not in any way manipulative, and does not entail taking something away from another person.

Rather, receiving from another is about a shifting, a shuttling back and forth between awareness of the external world, the gift and the giver, to your inner self, where you place, distribute and hold the gift. True receiving is an internal event, an opening of yourself like a child to a swing, or like God to a prayer. You bring nourishment from the outside in. If Ron is stroking my hand, I feel the touch, the sensation, whether I'm receiving it or not. The potential for the event ranges from insignificant to precious. It all depends on the spirit in which it was given and the capability of the receiver. I hold the power to make his touch impotent or nourishing; to take his touch from a mere physical contact, to something that maximizes the power of the gift and is satisfying and meaningful. I'm aware of him, his intentions, and his touch on the outside, and I allow his touch to permeate my skin into my whole being. I want to turn my skin and every pore into a sponge, receiving and appreciating every ounce of what I am being given. From the gift of this moment, I may feel safe and a sense of belonging, precious and loved, attractive and desired. And it doesn't have to be a big, obvious event. It can be done thoroughly, efficiently and effectively in the natural course of time. The ordinary moment can become a sweet, extraordinary moment of aliveness and healing.

To truly receive, you must remain focused on the experience of receiving. If you're thinking about your to-do list while making love, obviously you will not receive the full impact of the love and pleasure being offered. And you deny your lover the fulfillment of being received. If your mate tells you that you look pretty, and you respond with, "I think I look fat," you have taken the gift and effectively thrown it in the trash. You have given no effort to receiving. If someone is giving you words of love, and you can only let in a little bit, there is a loss on both sides.

A poignant example of restricted receptivity is from one of my workshops. A father, a brilliant astronomer, had been remote and uncommunicative throughout the life of his 23-year-old daughter. He spent his life in his basement lab, or peering at the sky. She was desperate for his attention and his affection, and was interpreting his remoteness as a reflection of his lack of love for her.

When I had gone as far as I could go with her in one-on-one therapy, I suggested she invite her father to a weekend workshop. She was totally overwhelmed by the idea, and could not imagine in a million years that he would be willing to do anything for her that was so far out of his comfort zone. I suggested she ask. To her shock and amazement, he agreed!

Wearing a trench coat, he arrived at the workshop—a pale, balding man with wire rim glasses. He stood in the opening circle of participants, stiff, with his head down and eyes on the floor, unable to give even the slightest eye contact to anyone. An entire day passed before he removed his coat. In what was, for him, an uncomfortable setting, it seemed to protect him. As person after person did work in front of the group, he began to soften and open. He became curious and interested. At times, he appeared deeply moved. Off came the raincoat. When his daughter revealed how she had felt abandoned by him all these years, he respectfully acknowledged his absence, and his discomfort with emotional closeness. He was now willing to learn.

I asked him to sit on the floor in front of her and gaze at his daughter, as he would a newly discovered star, and to experiment with integrating his heart in the process. When I asked him to report his findings, he spoke of noticing her beautiful, long, brown hair and lovely brown eyes. He found her to be precious, kind and vulnerable. And in his heart, there was a very deep love for her. With guidance, he broke through his inability to express his affection. Finally, after 23 years, he told his daughter how much he loved her. I asked the daughter how much of her father's love she was receiving in that moment—from zero to a 100 percent. She said 20 percent. Even when the love was staring her in the face, she couldn't receive it. Due to the many years she spent surviving in the absence of affection, she had not developed receptive capabilities. It was easier for her to live without love than it was to take it in.

The most important part of my work with this client was to train her in receptivity. Receiving is an activity. It requires purpose and concentration. It requires investing just as much focus on receiving as you want the other person to invest in giving. Receiving is creating and focusing on the awareness of your needs being met, and maximizing the impact of this sense of fulfillment. This capacity to receive well is essential to achieving both satiation and integration.

Try this brief experiment. Look around at your environment now and choose a color you are seeing that pleases you. Go inside your body and fill yourself with breath. Place your two feet on the floor. Feel the support of your backbone while you focus intently on that color. Is it a solid patch of blue or green, or are there as many variations in the shade of green as there are on certain leaves? Really look. See what is before you. Take in the beauty of the color. Wonder about it. Give gratefulness that this color, in this moment, is in the world for you. Receive it as a gift in your body.

The more you do it, the more you practice in a moment here or there, the sooner you will make healthy receptivity a way of life.

The Satiation Signal

Satiation is organic. Once you've thoroughly moved out and/or expressed yourself effectively, made good contact in the world and are in a state of heightened awareness that lets you receive what has been provided, you'll feel a sense of satisfaction within, the satiation signal—a feeling of that's enough, I'm full, no more, stop now, job complete. Experientially, it is as though a bell sounds in your brain, reverberates throughout your body, and announces that your hunger is satisfied. You're now satiated and free to move on.

This path to satiation could be called the *road to provision*. The journey of meeting and providing for your wants and needs requires not only an ability to move out and express them skillfully but also a willingness, even a generosity of spirit, in responding to those needs. Of course, satiation never could be reached without a well-honed capacity to receive what you are being given.

Strange as it may sound, I know many obese adults and children who feel hungry following a five-course dinner. They're unable to complete the movement of thorough chewing and tasting of food. Instead, they seem to swallow it whole. They don't feel a satiation signal. In some cases, there may be organic reasons why people don't experience satiation. In most instances, however, people are not concentrating on the entire process of eating. They're not awake to the chewing, the texture, the flavor, the changes in flavor as they continue chewing, their body swallowing the food, or the incremental awareness of becoming full. They take their first bite, and then seemingly go into a trance of unawareness. In essence, they're eating without being in contact with their food, and thus do not receive the nourishment and pleasure. They have no moment of "Boy, that was good!" or any sign of satiation.

Watch any act of discovery, such as a home run in baseball, or a moment of understanding and awareness, and you will see the outstretched hand, and the voice yelling, "Yes!" On an emotional level, imagine a distraught child running into the arms of a loving parent. In time, you can see the child's body relax, go limp and rest on the parent. Eventually, the sobbing subsides and comfort sets in. After the child organically perceives the satiation signal, he turns his attention to something new.

On an interpersonal level, you've had that difficult

conversation with your father, and you've said everything you've wanted to say in an effective way. He has heard your need for support and has responded compassionately. You've thoroughly experienced and received his love and connection. You part with an embrace, and feel a deep sense of relief and satisfaction. Your organism has signaled satiation.

Integration

Once you have experienced satiation, you're then charged with the job of integrating what has been provided and received, that is, assimilating it until it becomes an organic part of you. Integration is that time of reflection, discrimination, elimination, containment, digestion and assimilation. Your body does this quite naturally. Remember that glass of water we talked about? After you've moved out into the world to get it, you drank it to satiation. While you're reflecting on having quenched your thirst, your body is doing the physiological labor of thorough integration by delivering the fluid where it needs to go to regulate your health. It takes that water and distributes it to the rest of your body, where it hydrates, nourishes and assists with filtering and eliminating that which is not nourishing. By drinking the water, you provide for the exact needs of your organism. Consciously receiving it, and being aware of quenching your thirst, can be as short as "That was perfect; what's next?"

To continue the eating analogy, after you have received the food, and felt the satiation signal, it is time to fully assimilate what you have eaten. Hopefully, you have been aware of your body receiving pleasure throughout the process. Receiving is consciously taking in and allowing the food to fill, nourish and please you. Once the meal is complete, it's important to take a moment to review what you've eaten, how you've enjoyed it, how nourished you feel, and how your hunger has been satisfied. You may rate it, as a culinary experience, as the best ever or simply as comfort food. In all cases, receiving well ensures satiation, while the process of receptivity again is required for integration.

This need for reflection and receptivity is a process not totally understood in this Western "hurry up" culture. I've seen repeatedly children who have not been taught the importance of concentrating on eating and receiving their food. They're not doing the labor of focusing on, enjoying, or appreciating it. Instead, they experience constant craving and are strangers to the experience of satiation and integration. The whole fast food concept, with its emphasis on instant satisfaction, not only flies in the face of a healthy integration of the experience of eating, but also the potential for wholesome living.

Of course, we're talking about food here, but the same approach to chewing, swallowing, and digesting applies to all life experiences. Concentrate on them, chew on them, ingest what is nourishing, eliminate what isn't and receive and reflect on what you have been given.

Integration of an experience is the time to be in close conversation with yourself, and further absorb the precious moment you just created. Integration will require that you leave contact with the environment, or the interpersonal world, and enter into the intrapersonal environment. It is a time to review, discriminate, acknowledge and appreciate the action you've taken on your own behalf. It doesn't have to take long. "Great job, Mariah. Thank you. You're so welcome!"

Integration is also a time to discriminate between what is nourishing for you and what is not useful. This may necessitate some reconstruction of the original event; you tailor the experience to precisely fit the needs of your organism. This will involve evaluating and absorbing what about the experience was positive and nourishing while spitting out and eliminating what was toxic or not useful. In short, you take the best and leave the rest.

If your uncle Harry is unskilled at self-expression, and uses joking and sarcasm while trying to connect with you, you may need to acknowledge to yourself that his words may have stung, while it was also true that he was attempting to give you his positive regard and connection. Take in his love, and eliminate the sting of his delivery. His love is what you'll want to integrate and carry with you.

Try this experiment. Imagine someone smiling at you, or speaking to you with affection. Now concentrate on seeing that person giving to you. Consciously draw his gift into you by breathing and pulling the kindness and affection all the way down to your toes. When you feel full with the gift, shift your focus away from the giver back to yourself. Then reflect momentarily on what a sweet moment that was, and notice how you have been changed by it. Bathe your body in it for a bit. Take a final digestive breath, and then move on.

Exact moments of healing, which have the potential for positively changing the course of your life, usually require a more prolonged integration period. When my clients are finished a piece of work with me, they often arrive close to or at the satiation point by taking in and receiving as much as they are able at the moment. I encourage them to continue to feel the effects in their body, and to reflect upon what they've just created. I also counsel them to continue to think about the experience in the weeks ahead, and to focus on digesting and taking into themselves what was most productive and healing about it. This integration can be completed in a matter of minutes, days, months or years. As long as the moment of healing continues to provide something essentially necessary for you, then continue to remember it, chew on it and let it become part of you. Work it until you get out of it the last morsel of emotional.

Completion/Closure

When all the receiving, satiating, reflecting and integrating is finished, you're not done yet! Now you need to put the period at the end of the sentence. That's the moment when you feel your body breathe and say, "Done, complete, fini." It's a body experience. The screen quietly fades to black. It's not the jubilance that can come with satiation. The event is over, not with a bang, but a whimper. There might be a sense of relief that it's over. You have left no stone unturned; you are free and balanced. This is the goal of the organism—to complete the business at hand. It's called *closure*. You have successfully provided for your wants and needs.

Opening to New Experience

Once closure is achieved, the organism naturally shifts into a state of openness. You are ready to take on a new figure or a new piece of business. You are open to new sensory stimuli, moments, activities and interests.

Think now of the thirst analogy. After getting that glass of water, drinking it to satiation, and receiving and reflecting on it, you say something like, "That was good, perfect. Done. I needed that." Do you remember the next moment? What did you feel? What went through your mind and body? Did you turn and ask yourself, "Now what?" Or maybe you had something to do and said, "Ok, let me get to that." Then go to the next figure that emerges from the ground (background) of your experience.

It can be a pleasant emptiness when you can sense your organism, your body, at peace and beginning to feel an expanding current of interest. OK, I'm ready to take on what's next. What interests me? You have the energy to welcome and take on the new and the now. There's a feeling of absolute completeness and nothing left to be gratified. Momentarily, you are suspended from the tension of the hunger instinct. All the focus and labor of navigating through the cycle, and meeting the wants and needs, is over. You feel lighter; not preoccupied or burdened. You are in the now. Sometimes wide-eyed and bushy tailed. Sometimes quietly available for the next emerging need. You are in the moment and free from being under the influence of whatever it was that occupied you before. Colors may be brighter; sensations more keenly felt.

Sometimes the moment of openness is all too brief. If you can purposefully linger in it, you will experience a sense of wonder and looking around at your environment and your life. It's a time full of potential for heightened self-awareness, aliveness and excitement. It's the time before you select your next figure. During your selection process, you can wander from interest to interest deciding what most intrigues you. Abraham Maslow, an American psychologist, would call it a "peak experience," especially if, during your selection process, you include the standard of what will offer you the greatest sense of satisfaction, self-actualization or bliss.

Navigating Full Circle/You've Done It!

On a daily basis, whether you know it or not, you are moving continually around the Cycle of Awareness and Contact. You are shifting in your seat, quenching your thirst, embracing your children, choosing strawberry over vanilla, having those difficult conversations, scratching an itch, putting on a raincoat to get to the car. This gives you tantalizing proof that each time you go around the circle, you become more masterful in your life. Realization of these choices moves us from victim to responsible adult; from passive to active; from "I have to" to "I choose to." Mastering the art of navigating around the cycle can significantly transform your life.

In fact, for most of your life, you are successfully navigating around the cycle. You're now reading this book. If you've gone to a bookstore, you've driven home. You've opened this book. You've turned page after page to get to this sentence, all in response to a felt need. Hopefully, you'll take it in, become satiated, receive value, and sift through all the information to grasp the nuggets that matter to you. You may want to go back and re-read those passages that have impacted you most deeply, so that you may fully integrate what was valuable to you. Then you'll be open and ready to go on to a new experience.

Once this formula for healthy living is integrated within you, your stuck times become shorter, your insights deeper, and your skills honed. You are responding to the needs of your organism all the time. What you want is to live well, in a way that respects and responds to those needs without interruption and with a level of interpersonal and intrapersonal skill that maximizes your potential to achieve success in your life.

You may have a fresh start any moment you choose,
for this thing we call "failure" is not the falling down,
but the staying down.

—Mary Pickford

Chapter Three

POTHOLES ON THE ROAD TO PROVISIONS

In the course of living your life, you'll inevitably discover roadblocks, limitations and inabilities to create deep satisfaction. You may discover deficiencies in your capacity to express love, or to move out on your own behalf, or to form lasting friendships. When you find yourself stuck like this, you'll need to dive below the surface, into the deep of who you are and discover the unmet needs at the core of your dysfunction that are calling for correction and for exact moments of healing. I don't mean that your life should stop. You'll still be cycling around in many ways, while simultaneously looking for and creating opportunities for healing your deeper wounds.

We all fall, over and over again, in our own holes. We make fear-based decisions and cover our wounded hearts with defensive garb. If you want to know why your life isn't working, you need to understand the obstacles you place in your own way. I like to call them your sabotage techniques. They include behaviors such as procrastination, self-criticism, numbing yourself, distancing people. The list goes on. If you have a lot of unmet goals, that is indication enough that you are in need of some healthy adjustments to your way of living.

The journey around the Awareness and Contact Cycle often is interrupted by a myriad of conscious and unconscious resistances. It is not easy to fully embody the truth of who we are, and present the longings of our being with transparency and skill. Anytime we get stuck at any point along the cycle, we create baggage called *unfinished business*, which becomes one of many unmet needs that we store in the warehouse of our being—think millstone around our necks. Do you want to line your shelves with skill, completed tasks and well-satisfied needs, or with a weighty accumulation of unresolved issues, incomplete relationships and lost dreams?

It is critically important to navigate the full breadth of the cycle with purposeful attention and action. Anytime you successfully arrive at completion, and restore balance to your organism, you can begin the cycle again with one less piece of unfinished business. Why is this so important? Because it's this unfinished business that, when accumulated, can weigh you down with a myriad of symptoms: depression, frustration, anxiety, poor self-esteem and relationship failure.

Unfinished Business

Unfinished business is created by getting stuck at any juncture in the cycle, causing "old stuff" to get in the way and contaminate new experiences. Maybe you were unaware of how you felt in certain situations or what you needed, or maybe you didn't say what needed to be said. Maybe you were unable, or unwilling, to express what you wanted or to move out on your own behalf when you needed to. Or maybe you were ineffective in your communications with someone you hold dear, discovered what you needed, and didn't go for it, or weren't able to take in and appreciate what you've accomplished when you did. All of these are disabilities that impair the quality of your life and can continue to accumulate, preventing you from approaching a new situation clean and clear of the past.

For example, if you had a toxic relationship with your mother that you never healed, chances are those unhealed aspects of your relationship will show up in your subsequent family relationships with your spouse or children. If you were abused or treated poorly by an authority figure, and you never dealt with those feelings and achieved some internal resolution, you'll carry those authority issues over into adult life.

Ron has said that his day was unproductive if he had an unpleasant discussion with one of our sons in the morning before they rushed off to school. He couldn't wait until they came home so that he could complete the conversation or clear up some miscommunication that may have occurred in the hurriedness of the morning. Sometimes small issues can stay with us all day, making it impossible to be effective until they are resolved.

Getting Stuck

In fact, many of the symptoms that people bring into a

psychotherapy office can be attributed to *stuckness* at specific points of the cycle. Although my own approach sees people's patterns of behavior as looking for health rather than as pathological symptoms, it is worth noting some of these syndromes, and their relationship to the cycle.

For example, a trauma victim who dissociates out of a need to avoid sensations in his body, or a catatonic schizophrenic who literally freezes his body into immobility, is stuck between stimulus and energetic formation. The feelings generated by the stimulus may be too painful to tolerate and thus the person doesn't reach a clear energetic formation. The client may stay numb, rigid and unfeeling. People who suffer from attention deficit disorder (ADD) have a hard time focusing long enough on any one stimulus to have any completion about it. They are barraged with many stimuli and many little and large pieces of unfinished business. They stay distracted by the pull of multi-stimuli, and have a hard time getting all the way around the cycle, sometimes even in small tasks.

In today's technological world, frequently there is a problem of being bombarded by too many external stimuli. This can cause anxiety and discomfort, because it's impossible to immediately attend to so many stimuli. Young people often are writing homework assignments while watching television, listening to an ipod and instant-messaging friends. The skill of multi-tasking demands that one respond efficiently to incoming stimuli. In fact, you never are doing two things at once. You are shifting back and forth between stimuli.

The downside to chronic multi-tasking may be the inability to fully attend in depth to one issue at a time, or to sustain contact with one stimulus long enough to have a complete and satisfying experience. This is a common problem with people diagnosed with ADD. They have difficulty staying with one stimulus long enough to experience a clear feeling (energetic formation), or to achieve satisfaction. Constantly jumping from one figure to another, they leave some projects incomplete and procrastinate starting others. Easily distracted and carried away by multiple stimuli, their progress chronically is interrupted and, therefore, they have difficulty ever achieving completion. The skill of focusing is what they desperately need to learn. They are stuck.

Those who have a lot of feelings, that is, lots of energetic formations, may not know what to do with those feelings. They don't know the next question to ask is, "What do you need to do about that feeling?" Furthermore, they may not have been allowed to have needs as a young child. They may walk into my office full of so-called "free-floating anxiety," as if it were the result of no particular stimulus. If I ask them what they need, they look incredulous, or afraid. The question is out of their familiarity or comfort zone. They and their lives have been stuck at the energetic formation juncture.

There are people who clearly know what they want or need and, because of some fear or conditioning, they will not express their desire or move out on their own behalf. They're stuck at having wants or needs, with nowhere to go with them. These people are prone to depression and chronic unmet longings.

Others can move out and express themselves but not well enough to achieve completion or satisfaction. They might be withholding, indirect or held back, complaining or criticizing instead of requesting. They may have a conduct disorder. They come in with job, marriage or relationship failure, because of their inadequacy in making contact in the world.

Then there are those who seem to have it all—success, a lovely family—yet, for some reason, they have chronic dissatisfaction and depression. They're prone to sabotaging it all. They don't feel worthy, and/or able, to receive their good fortune in life. There are people who give and give and give to home, family, charities and neighbors yet feel empty; drained, alone, unappreciated and unworthy, no matter how many times they are told how wonderful they are. They are colanders. They can't receive and retain. All the good stuff drains out through the holes.

We all can get stuck at any point along the Awareness and Contact Cycle. And we all have our places where we are more likely to get stuck. What matters is that you become aware of where you are stuck, respond by dedicating yourself to healing the old wounds that are in the way, and develop new skills of healthy living.

Resistances to Authentic Contact

We back up, sidestep, and talk around and around the point. We dart our eyes, turn a cold shoulder, or become the joker. My son,

Cole, uses a very diplomatic suggestion. "Will you call me tomorrow, Mom?" instead of, "I want to hang up now. I have more interesting things to do." Why? Because we don't want to be in touch with what's precisely going on. We don't want to engage. We want to avoid the subject, spare the pain, or as in Cole's case, we have better things to do.

Sometimes we're aware of what we're doing. Often we're not. We don't mean to blow off our friends, or whitewash the pain of a spouse, or neglect our children because we're uncomfortable with emotional closeness. The underlying reason for our behavior often is below the surface of our awareness. Frequently, it has to do with avoiding discomfort.

In short, these resistances are what we use to avoid authentic contact. They probably were used originally for a self-protective purpose—the avoidance of potential pain at some point in your life. However, under the heading of "that was then and this is now," in adult life, instead of meeting new experiences afresh, resistances often serve to limit our authentic contact with one another and isolate us.

Let's talk about six of our most commonly used resistances to contact. They're so important that I invite you to see if you recognize yourself in them. And, rather than being self-critical, learn about them with an attitude of, "Ah, isn't that interesting about me."

Introjection/Swallowing Whole

When you swallow something whole—a concept, a belief, a story someone tells you—you're introjecting. You're treating a solid like a liquid, swallowing instead of chewing.

Cops are good. Cops are bad. Catholics are the only ones who go to heaven. Jews are the chosen people. Muslims are fanatics. Boys want only one thing. Republicans don't know what they're talking about. Nice guys finish last. No one will ever love you. Pretty girls are thin. You're ugly. You'll never amount to anything.

There's no end to the distortions we're all asked to swallow.

Introjections, in the extreme, can be life threatening. Think of a prisoner of war, or a cult victim, who is held captive and brainwashed. It takes very skilled interventions to deprogram people who have been victims. Think of the beautiful model who spends her life obsessing about being too fat, unattractive, not perfect enough. Bulimia and anorexia are rampant among young women; often they are fueled by vicious introjects from the media. Whole lives are ruined when these indigestible foreign bodies dominate a person's existence.

Projection/Imaginings

Take a moment to think about how often you imagine what other people are thinking or feeling. Based on your imaginings, you make some decisions about how you want to interact or not with that person. Projection, another resistance to contact, occurs when you attribute feelings or qualities to someone else when they really belong to you. Frequently, I tell my students to always remember that they know nothing about another person. This is especially important for highly intuitive people. You must inquire to know the truth. You can know what you see—a smile, a tear, tightened fists—and you can guess what they mean. But you won't be accurate all the time. You must inquire: "I see you are crying, and I imagine you're feeling sad." The experience of yawning often makes me teary. If someone asks me what's wrong, they're assuming sadness or upset. A benign moment, no doubt, and still inaccurate. Be humble. Inquire. Be a constant student.

In this era of new age thinking, we are bombarded by intuitives and psychics proclaiming to know the truth about people. I have no doubt there are some legitimate, gifted people with extraordinarily keen vision and perception. In fact, I've met a few of them. But the vast majority are projectors, let loose on the general population. Beware.

In my first job as a social worker, I imagined for two weeks that my boss was angry with me. I finally got up the nerve to ask him why he was angry with me. He looked totally bewildered. For him, the question came out of left field. I immediately woke up to the fact that it was I who was angry with him. I had totally projected my feelings onto him. Fritz Perls estimates that we project 90% of the time. A cornfield will look like a business to a farmer, a future goldmine to a developer, a playground to a child, and a hideaway to lovers.

Deflection/Avoiding the Intensity

If you can't stand the heat of contact, get out of life's kitchen. This could be the motto for deflectors. We've all met deflectors and probably sometimes behave like them. They're the ones who use humor, who stonewall, who talk around or change the subject, who talk too much or too little or who say anything that avoids the intensity of being fully present and authentic with another person in the present moment. They minimize, intellectualize and rationalize.

They're the people who are afraid of intimacy, and intensity of feelings, and often imagine rejection or hurt. A client of mine recently was discussing his wife and her pattern of deflecting by creating distance and animosity soon after they were close and intimate. She was unable to maintain a healthy level of intimacy, so she would repeat the cycle, "Come close. Go away."

Dr. John Gottman, in his groundbreaking research and book, *What Makes Marriages Succeed, and What Makes Them Fail,* says that the single most powerful predictor of divorce is a husband stonewalling or refusing to engage in conflict with his wife. The wife may reach out to present an issue or solve a problem and the husband deflects her attempts either by changing the subject, or effectively redirecting the conversation to another issue. When I work with a spouse like this, I'll teach him to use the phrase, "Tell me more," and to breath and support himself while his partner speaks her mind. Good relationships are not devoid of conflicts. Rather than avoid contact with a loved one, learn to stay present while having healthy disagreements. Develop your capacity to emotionally meet and engage with people, while avoiding destructive interactions.

Confluence/Flowing With

Confluence comes from the Latin word, *confluere,* meaning to flow with. Go along to get along. Usually, there is a spoken or unspoken agreement with a person, organization or social group demanding confluence, such as, obedience, squashing of your needs to meet their needs in exchange for something, be it belonging, acceptance, love, money, security. Those who demand confluence feel entitled to have it their way. They can be guilt-provoking, controlling, and even dominating. They hold the power, show righteous indignation and often are punitive when their confluent partners don't behave according to their agendas.

Certainly, there are times in life, marriage or parenting when our individual concerns must be postponed for the sake of a child, spouse, family or basketball team, for that matter. However, those caught in confluence generally sell their souls for the protection or resources they need. They lose themselves in the relationship and feel guilty if they stray from their agreement, most often blaming themselves.

I have a client who has been totally subservient to her husband for the past 10 years. She allows him to dominate all decisions about the home, child rearing, and social activities. At the same time, she swallows his many criticisms of her. Yes dear, yes dear, yes dear. When her child began having symptoms of poor self-esteem and failure in social relationships, she took him to a therapist who suggested she do her own therapy. She quickly discovered that her confluence with her husband was an exchange for marriage, security, and a family. She hadn't thought she was worthy of a man's love. The process of recovery will involve her reclaiming her true identity, feelings and needs, as she learns the skills of authentic contact.

Retroflection/The Boomerang

Retroflectors can be their own best friend, or their own worst enemy. They are their own Santa Claus, lover and confidante. Often, retroflectors make themselves their own target and adversary. In either case, they do to themselves what they would like to do to or with another person. Usually suffering from deep insecurity and damaged self-esteem, they resist authentic contact in the world.

Perhaps fearing rejection or fearing being controlled, they cannot risk loving someone else. So they often turn their affection inward and retreat to a life of narcissism and self-protection. We're not talking about healthy self-love here. We're talking about someone who substitutes self-indulgence for healthy positive contact.

I love me; I think I'm grand.
I sit in the movies and hold my hand.

Others are unable to express their anger in positive healthy ways, so they turn their aggression inward and implode. They clench their teeth, pound their thighs, bite their nails to the quick, pick their face, pull out their hair, and cut their bodies. They're prone to headaches, depression, cancer, and digestive and posture problems. I know a woman whose voice sounds like a perpetual growl. I know she carries unhealed and undelivered anger every day. Again, the body takes the hit.

Proflection/False Gift

False flatterers proclaim their love in grand style, and are resentful when it's not returned in kind. Their generosity is more like making an unspoken deal. Let me give you a present today, so you'll give me one tomorrow. Proflection, a new resistance recently identified by Sylvia Crocker, a Gestalt therapist and trainer, is an indirect way of caring for your needs. Proflectors don't ask for what they want directly; they try to control or seduce you to get it, hoping you'll get the hint or read their minds. You might be excited when they say, "I love you." But what they really want is to hear you say, "I love you." They avoid the direct contact, the vulnerability of revealing their needs while depriving themselves of the joy that comes from true generosity and heartfelt giving.

Desensitization/Checking Out

Have you ever felt really down, and used alcohol, drugs, food, cigarettes, cynicism or overwork to numb yourself? Have you ever had sex and missed it? Have you ever been in a situation that you wish you were not in and resorted to daydreaming to escape the discomfort of being where you were? If so, you have desensitized yourself. Sometimes it works for us. Maybe the meeting was pretty boring. However, desensitization is a vehicle for avoiding sensations and/or feelings in your body. It's another way of avoiding full contact with yourself, others and your environment. At its worst, desensitization can take the form of addiction or severe dissociation, an altered personality state that separates a person from present experience.

Some people grow up in a family or culture that is uneasy with the physical and emotional aspects of life. They look like they're not at home in their bodies nor comfortable in their own skin. With little body awareness or sensation, they're like walking heads with no aliveness from the neck down.

Sometimes, we see this phenomenon with sexual trauma victims who numb themselves, effectively amputating their genitals. Because the pain of abuse is associated with that area of the body, they want to avoid it at all costs. They have the experience of leaving their bodies behind, moving on to a safer place and thus avoiding contact. In the past, desensitization usually worked for them. It may have helped them survive their abuse. "If I'm numb, it won't hurt." However, if they stay numb, they sabotage any possibility for real and nourishing intimacy.

Avoidance of contact is not always a destructive thing. Sometimes there is wisdom in it. What is most important is to learn how and when you are resisting contact, and then explore your motivations—conscious and unconscious. The goal is to make aware choices instead of having your life be watered down by your runaway discomfort with contact. This habitual turning away leads us to a life less lived.

Good Medicine

Discovering roadblocks that you unconsciously or consciously employ is a major step toward health. You've learned about numerous ways to get yourself stuck thereby sabotaging your progress in life. As you work on undoing these resistances, you'll need courage and compassion. Remember, originally you used these resistances to protect yourself, however dysfunctional and outdated they now have become. Respect your resistances. Understand the intention behind them, and compassionately retrain yourself in more productive skills. You will not eliminate resistances; you will retire or transform them, always with an appreciative heart.

Behind your resistances are wounds that have not yet healed— wounds calling for attention and good medicine. As you provide exact moments of healing, one after another, your need to utilize old fear-based behaviors will lessen, and your capacities for health will grow.

Salvation was served in a popover. My heart of steel melted with the
butter. It was our ritual. My mother, drenched in guilt. I, steeled in
silence on the top, bubbling hot at the bottom. Molten lava with no
way to spew. What mattered was that she got up, wrenched herself
from her bed of oblivion. Even standing was precarious. Then comic
relief when she walked, angling forward like some ambulatory tower
of Pisa with her hair standing straight out as if she had been
plugged into a socket. She was sick with old drink, yet her love
made her rise up, stumble her way to the kitchen to make popovers.
Somewhere near the third bite came the moment. Redemption for
her. Salvation for me. Hell would happen again.
Yet in that moment, we tasted freedom.

—Mariah Fenton Gladis

Chapter Four

CREATING EXACT MOMENTS OF HEALING

I was in a supermarket. I remember an African-American boy about age 7, trying to get a bottle of soda off the shelf. He dropped it, and it exploded all over the floor. Eyes of terror looked up at me. At 22 years old, I stood frozen. I couldn't move; I didn't move. It wasn't that I didn't care. I just didn't do anything. Now, when I remember that moment, I think about how I didn't make him my business. I maintained the boundary of, "You're not my responsibility even though my heart goes out to you." When I remember this moment, I wish I could go back to the supermarket in that exact moment and help him. I want to kneel down at eye level and tell him it's fine, that I've done that too, and then help him negotiate with the supermarket manager. Show him how to do that. If they are holding him accountable, give him money. I learned from that moment, and I would never behave in the same way again.

Why does the moment with that beautiful child repeat itself in my memory? Because we locked eyes? Because he was black? I can't say for sure. I see those little brown eyes, and worry about what I taught him. How could I not have helped him? For me, it could have been a moment of satisfaction; a time when I contributed something significant to another person; when I met the moment head on with full capacity to provide. Instead, I merged with the trauma response, and became paralyzed, made my exit instead of my entrance. It was, and still is, indigestible to my system. With his eyes, he asked for help. I'm afraid that his memory will be that of my back walking away in his moment of need.

I can say for sure he was my teacher. I learned it's not enough to feel compassion. I must move out on my compassion, and put it into action. I missed the moment for my healing, and his, and it's interesting that my life would become about providing these moments of healing in other people's lives.

Although this was a single, brief incident in my life, it gave me a jolt, a wake-up call, a clear window into how I needed to grow. I know you have heard the phrases, "It's too late; it happened; it's over; grow up; get over it." And you may have said that to yourself at one time or another. Well, get over that idea. It's wrong, wrong, wrong.

You are a magnificently designed creature; the creator made you incredibly perfect, not flawless. It's never too late to go back to any moment in your life to relive, rewrite or re-create it in the exact way you want it to be in the present. Everyone has moments that haunt them. Heal those moments! They can become so imbedded in your being that they begin to shape your every thought and action. They become your master rather than you mastering them. So much time is wasted recounting, recollecting, bemoaning—time that could be used for providing. Make that moment of healing happen.

Unlike Superman, who was not allowed to interfere with the course of history, you *must* take the hero's journey back in time. If you have a haunting memory, a recurring problem or an aching need that remains unfulfilled, it will stick in your gut with the strength of a bear. You can't wish it away, deny it, erase it, wave fingers in front of your eyes at it or muscle your way through it. You must forage through the rubble to find the burning need at the heart of the matter. If not, an inner voice will haunt you with the demand, "Pay attention to me. I need you. I cannot change until you take care of me." You must go back.

If you listen carefully to this voice, you can hear the truths that lie at the core of your "stuckness," your immobility and inability to evolve gracefully. They whisper secrets of vulnerability that you have hidden from yourself, such as, "Until I am held in the arms of a loving father, I cannot open my heart to any man," or "I will never trust authority until I hear an admission of fault and an apology from the teacher who molested me," or "I'll never be able to lose weight until I am fed and nurtured by a joyful mother." In all cases, you must discover what went wrong, what is missing and what is needed and then provide it. These exact moments of healing must be purposeful and precisely tailored. They must respond to deeply felt needs that neither destiny nor the individual has yet healed.

Life Moments—Hurtful and Healing

When I have the luxury of time in a long workshop or in an ongoing therapeutic process in my office, I ask clients to make a year-by-year life inventory of their most influential memories and people, both positive and negative. Through this self-examination they can identify sources of strength as well as any impeding unfinished business. All their moments or memories, dear and painful, have accumulated over time and molded them into who they are today. The purpose of the inventory is to discover where they are stuck in order to determine what exact moments are needed for their recovery.

In your memory bank, there are the best moments—moments that are pearls you treasure because they positively affected your life and continue to nurture you each time you recall them. These are the memories that slip into your consciousness when you need strength and hope. They fill you with their sweet warmth—your body tingles, your heart swells and you may shed meaningful tears. They inspire you to carry on. Some of them are monumental, some minute. The birth of a child, a marriage, fishing with father, laughter shared with cherished friends, a child's first steps—all of these precious memories make indelibly intimate marks on your soul.

There have been many precious moments with my husband, and two sons, when I've wished I could stop time to preserve forever the joy of sharing their lives. I am sure that you, too, have cherished moments with those you love. You must remember them and carry them with you always, as a source of strength and hope. Moments are what you have. Treasure them.

Then, there are the worst moments. These are the central focus of my professional work. These are the times that Thomas Paine said "Try men's souls." These are the memories that haunt you; these are the ones that replay in your psyche, not to give you pleasure but instead to drag you back to places you never want to revisit. They can be moments dropped, without warning, like a bomb: the accidental death of a loved one, a friend's suicide, the diagnosis of a terminal disease. They can be moments that never should have been allowed to occur, such as moments of violence and sexual abuse.

As a therapist, I have heard cries of human agony, gruesome accounts of incidents that have seriously damaged people's lives. They always stun me, and I am momentarily suspended in denial. I wonder how it is that we humans can inflict such pain on one another, pain that often is directed to the ones we are supposed to love the most.

You also may experience damaging moments that are not as intense, but still haunt you. These are moments when, perhaps, you wish you had made a different choice: when you hurt a friend, behaved counter to your sense of morality and fairness or said harsh words that you wish you could take back. You can carry the guilt of these moments for many years. And, who among us is free enough from guilt to cast the first stone?

All of these trying life moments can be so damaging that they stunt your development. You carry them in your eyes, on your face, in your posture, in the very fiber of your being and behavior. There's hardly an organ or emotion that escapes the fallout of their traumatic effects. They become diseases. Negatively charged body memories also can be triggered by seemingly unrelated events. And whether you are conscious of it or not, those memories carry with them the same terror, rage or humiliation as the original pain. These moments can cripple you with limiting beliefs: "I should have. Why did I? Why didn't I? If only I had. I need to forget and move on." We've all placed these judgments on ourselves, or had others do it for us.

Before "waking up" to self-awareness, you're often a passive recipient of your moments. Certainly in childhood, most of your moments happened to you. You were little and dependent and adults were the big people who had all the power. As an adult, you can still be a victim of circumstances beyond your control. However, in general, as an adult, you have more control over your destiny and you have the ability to respond to crises in a variety of ways.

As you gain more self-awareness and skill, you have more choices. Become the artist of your own moments. Approach each day as a painter to an empty canvas. Too few of us are fully aware of that privilege and responsibility. We do not realize the inherent power of actively choosing to create experiences moment-by-moment. Rather, we cling to the passive notion that life happens to us, that we are either helpless victims or "lucky ducks."

Configuration of Needs

When we go through a trauma (an extensive chronically injurious experience that is severe and devastating), that trauma or history will be a recurring stimulus in our foreground. It's an external stimulus, something from the environment that comes at us, and assaults us in some way emotionally, physically, spiritually. There is a huge reaction inside; it is almost always fight, flight or freeze.

In the moment of traumatic impact, the part of the brain that sequences time, the Broca's area, shuts down. Your ability to verbalize your experience also ceases. You become stuck in that moment. There is no exit, no felt moment of it being complete or over. Many people develop post traumatic stress syndrome, and a multitude of incidents can trigger the original traumatic stress response.

Also, at the time of the traumatic event and in the time immediately following the event, what I call a *configuration of needs* is formed around that trauma. If there is no repair, no provisional response from the environment, the configuration grows over time.

For instance, a person who has been raped may experience a number of organismic needs: to escape, to express repressed or unexpressed feelings, to be rescued, to have justice prevail, to experience compassion from important others, and so on. Each person is unique in his or her needs. Most people who have been through trauma are unaware of their exact personal configuration of needs, and of the importance of having each of these needs met in order to experience full healing and completion. The longer a person goes without any response to his or her needs, the more expanded the configuration becomes. If, for example, a person hides in shame for years, afraid to reveal the trauma, that isolation and lack of authentic contact with others, creates longing, loneliness, more fear, and so on. In a situation of chronic severe traumatic abuse, you can understand that the configuration is reinforced and grows more than in a single event.

In my work, I am trying to understand and heal these configurations and precisely address those needs one by one. It is unlikely that any one piece of work can meet the whole configuration of needs. Nevertheless, it is important to be precise in discovering a person's needs and in creating exact corrective moments of healing. Any one piece of work can respond to more than one need but usually not all.

Each person's configuration is unique. There are no two people on the planet who need exactly the same thing. In general, you need the same *kinds* of things, the specific flavors and amounts of which vary. You might require a moment where you need a rescue from abusers. So, for example, we might create a rescue moment for you. Now, actively rejecting abuse is one piece of your configuration. There are other pieces. That's what I want you to be thinking about. What are your unmet wants and needs? They are in each person's life. It doesn't have to be a traumatic life to necessitate corrective moments. Everyone has unmet wants and needs that are specific to them.

If you have been slimed with shaming or have been sexually abused, you might need a moment of cleansing. You might need it more than one time. The real challenge is to very clearly and comprehensively understand your damaging unmet needs, then set about purposefully meeting them. Some of you can do it on your own. If you need to believe that there are friendly, kind people in the world then go out, walk, smile, watch, observe, look for evidence of kindness, and bring it to your attention. It is all around. You need to focus your attention on bringing it into a clear figure in your foreground awareness.

A configuration of needs often lies frozen in time, stuck in its irresolution, draping around you like an all-too-heavy coat of armor. Once you have created or received an important moment of healing, one of those old unmet needs is conjoined with, and linked to, a healthy corrective experience in the world, so that it is not remembered in isolation in the same way ever again. Linked to it is this moment of repair. Not that it won't hurt, but it will have less and less power and pain over time because the new experience now is connected to the trauma. The unmet need will recede into the background as new life emerges into the foreground.

As, one by one, the needs in the configuration are addressed and met, they begin adding to the constellation of wisdom and skills that become available, now and always. Think of a dark and empty sky as your configuration of needs. Now, continue to add stars to it over time, until the bright stars of healing moments dominate your night. In short, an ever-present, timeless constellation.

Better yet, the more healing moments you create, the more points of light you have. Even the memory of the exact moment of healing reinforces the healing. Every time you remember your exact moment of healing you strengthen it and add a new moment of healing. By recalling and repeating the moment of healing, you integrate the experience and create a new moment of healing, which is then added to the constellation. Eventually, you're going to outweigh it! A starry sky replaces the darkness.

You might ask how long this takes. Everyone is different. The more traumas you have, the more work you have to do. And for those people who repair enormous trauma, it's like climbing a mountain; the higher the climb, the more able the climber. Those who reach the summit have an enormous reservoir of skill and strength, and often are called upon to be leaders.

Creating Moments of Healing

Jason, a handsome, 30ish gay man arrived at a workshop despondent. For three days, he remained remote from the group, until he finally took his turn to work. As he relayed a story of being left by yet another partner, his blue eyes filled with tears. He expressed with great and solemn certainty that this was his last chance at love. He simply could not endure the pain again. After expressing his wrenching and life-threatening despair (via someone in the group sitting in for his partner), his body seemed to curl around itself, with head hung down and back arched. His shoulders were pressing forward, and I imagined if they could, they would have closed around him like wings. He was finished with love.

After his great release of sorrow, I felt it was not safe to leave him at that juncture. He needed to rise up. I designed an exact moment of healing that provided an experience of empowerment and resiliency. Still able-bodied at the time, I chose to play physically, offering some redeeming moments of tragic-comedy relief. I had the group pile 30 large pillows in the middle of the floor, and asked Jason to stand with his back to the mound, and to take a fall. He fell like a totem pole, straight and rigid, and lay there immobile and resigned. I told him to get up slowly, and to be aware of every miniscule motion involved in the act of standing.

On his feet, and face to face with me, I surprised him by pushing him back onto the pillows. He got the point, and slowly raised himself up. And again I knocked him down. We began having fun with it, as did the group. Everyone laughed. Although he was now ready for me, I surreptitiously hooked my right leg behind his knees—down he went again. This time loosely, laughing and doing a backward summersault to get up. Life color flushed his face. And I wasn't done yet. While I verbally teased him about his ability to take a fall and get up, we shifted weight on our feet from right to left like a pair of primitive dancers. While he was trying to avoid my right leg hooking him again, I hooked him with my left. Down he went. The group roared, and so did he. His smile and flexibility returned. His body opened, he jumped up and spontaneously said, "I can do this. I can take a fall and get up." After turning with outstretched arms for the group to see, he gave me a heartfelt bear hug.

"Never again," had turned into, "Well, maybe," and then into, "Yes, I can." Jason had learned resiliency. His exact moment of healing was delivered not through words or advice. Instead, it was provided through the wisdom of experience, which was grounded in his body.

Exact moments of healing are moments that produce substantial shifts in people's worldview, character and capacity to create meaningful contact with themselves, others and their environment. When creating exact moments of healing, a painful life experience or memory is recreated to include a positive healing outcome. You extend in time what has been frozen in time. By influencing and reconstructing destructive memory, and its effect on your organism and by merging it with a positive, corrective, healing experience, you can realize a deeper, precise and more complete healing. When you relive damaging moments in this active way, they no longer control you. They never again have the same toxic power in your life because they no longer will be remembered only as an agony. Now, a painful memory is accompanied by a healing memory. They exist side-by-side.

Once this merger of pain and healing takes place, a dysfunctional memory can never again be recalled in isolation because it is now forever bonded to a positive, healing memory. Old repetitive pathways of thinking are scrambled, and new healthier pathways have sprouted. The victim is beginning the mastery over that damaging moment, and taking the opportunity to reach out to a responsive, skillful, therapeutic environment. The positive revision is underway.

Professionally Designed Moments

I facilitate exact moments of healing at the point on the *Awareness and Contact Cycle* after the client has identified her Want/Need, but before Movement Expression to Satiation has occurred.

Later chapters describe case studies in which I co-create uniquely tailored exact moments of healing. Each professionally designed exact moment of healing is custom crafted to complete the *unfinished business* (issues or relationships needing attention and resolution) of each client. By correcting any negative moments that lie at the root of a client's dysfunction, these exact moments of healing are what make therapy work. They make us whole again.

If you are going to heal, you need something very specific that, up until now, has not been satisfied by any amount of support, talking, emotional release or problem-solving strategies. Many therapists lovingly encourage their clients to go back and get in touch with their pain. Being listened to by a sympathetic other is a necessary part of the recovery process; however, it often doesn't reach and remedy the deep, dark places within us. Many traditional therapies don't take the client the extra experiential mile and fill in the gaping holes. They talk around the unmet need and never get to the heart of the matter. They encourage adjustment to a bad situation rather than offering an antidote.

Many created exact moments of healing require substantial emotional and spiritual preparation and full participation in an ongoing therapeutic process co-created by the client and the therapist. The client must be ready to examine the moments that impair his capacity to live a productive, fully loving, intrapersonal and interpersonal life. And the therapist has to be equipped to fully meet the challenges that are presented. Without this level of commitment and capacity, you risk repeating your history and remaining stuck in your emotional pathology. That's not to say that everyone needs psychotherapy. There are some people with less traumatic histories who can create their own exact moments of healing without the help of a trained professional. We'll talk more about this later. Each journey is unique and truly a work in progress.

The Discovery Process

One important concept can be summed up in a basic principle, "Let's discover what you need and provide it." I work with people to illuminate memories, themes and problems that chronically impede their ability to lead healthy and fulfilling lives. As we trace the source of each issue, I prepare clients to return, to relive and to rewrite their histories until they are able, perhaps for the first time, to truly face their original pain. Then people co-construct their own remedy, and take responsibility for their own history, by rewriting it, empowering themselves for a future unobstructed by incomplete experiences.

There are seemingly small incidents that may require a corrective moment. You need to be the subjective evaluator of which events, which moments in your life, require continuation and completion. There may be some hurtful moments that you can tolerate without self-damage. You are the one who knows what events in your past are in your way and contributing to unhealthy patterns of loving and living.

The Power of the Group

Most often, I create exact moments of healing within a training or workshop setting, to provide the client with more people, more positive energy and a safe social environment.

There are several layers of group dynamics operating in every workshop. The first step requires all to agree to serve the person doing the work. The client's trust in the group and me is critical. Safety within the group is a crucial issue as well. In order to establish it, we move slowly in the beginning, offering exercises that help people to get to know and trust one another. Most importantly, we set down protective rules about anger and sexuality and we ask that everyone be committed to paying heartfelt attention to each member and honoring confidentiality.

Everyone in the room must be open to being moved and changed in the process. When we work this way, you can learn things about yourself that you may never have learned had you not witnessed the healing process of others. Group work of this nature can stimulate memories, and give you courage to face issues that you may never have faced. It teaches you how to open your arms and hearts to others in need. It's beautiful, for instance, to watch a father, who for years was unable to hold his young child and express love for him to now fully embrace that same adult child with his arms, heart and voice.

I once held the Gestalt position that you have to support yourself exclusively, and that to involve the environment in your healing was somehow less than "kosher." I don't believe that any more. We are social beings who need one another. True, you must initially learn to provide for your own needs, and to love yourself unconditionally. From that position, you can then invite other people into your life, to assist you in filling in the blanks of your history, to join you in finishing your unfinished business, and to applaud and support you as you move on; in short, to grow into a healthy interdependence.

I often think of the biblical phrase, "When two or more are gathered together, there is God." When I apply this to what we are doing in the workshops, it's clear that when two or more are gathered together with the intention of love and healing, there is transformational power far beyond what individuals in the room could create on their own. From where I sit, I know that the work is holy and that I am privileged to serve as its facilitator.

Music

Personally, I have used music since I was a child to help me express my feelings and to provide me with comfort, encouragement and a release. It was a natural transition, then, to bring music into my professional work, even though, in the early 1970s, it was unusual to use music at all and particularly to use it the way I did and still do.

Music is medicine for the soul, a pathway to the heart. The Ogallala Sioux have a saying, "Song is the breath of life that consecrates the act of living." It touches me, and most of us, on a kinesthetic level that nothing else can match. It can express for people what they are unable to express for themselves. Lyrics plus melody help set mood and tone. They can be a connector for all members of the group, each responding to the same stimulus, each in his or her own way

My friend, Jim, a record producer, says that music has a magical and mystical way of restoring inner harmony. I use music throughout the workshops, primarily to touch the hearts and souls of the people present, and to create a warm, emotional ambiance that enhances a participant's ability to open and go deeper. Music can stimulate memories, longings, repressed feelings; it can promote awareness of unfinished business, and reach you in places the spoken word cannot.

From a vast collection of music from every genre, I select specific pieces of music for each client, with the precise purpose of matching the spirit of the moment with the mood of the music. Have you ever heard a song on the radio and found yourself dropping unexpected tears because of some emotion that was stimulated? Do you know how a certain song can trigger memories of a moment or a time in your life? Music not only can help you access aspects of yourself you may have long forgotten, but also can help you enhance qualities of yourself that are not yet fully developed. A woman in the workshop felt she was a remote mother. I asked her to pick someone in the room to represent one of her children. I then asked her to cradle that child in her lap, while I played a very touching song called "Apple of My Eye" by Rosalie Sorrels. At first, her body was awkward and stiff. But, in time, and with my coaching, she softened and said she felt for the first time what it was like to actually nourish her child. She lost her mother at age 2, and had no memory of being held by her mother. When used therapeutically, as in this case, music not only can stimulate new growth, but also can anchor an experience into your being.

What's Important?

To give each client what he or she most needs, I initially ask, "What's important?" and then intently watch and listen. I observe how clients hold their bodies. I listen to their tones of voice and the details of their stories. I inquire and wait like a photographer in a dark room for the precise image of their needs to arise from the developing solution and come clearly into focus. Based on what has been revealed, I then suggest and create (never coerce) "experiments," or experiences that facilitate a client's ability to "move out" and express what he wants or needs in ways that will maximize the potential for satisfaction and completion.

Throughout my complete interaction with a client, I open myself to fully empathize with what he is feeling while still holding onto my professional thought process and creativity. This is a very delicate balance. If I stand too far back, and do not use myself as a person with full emotions, I'll withhold something precious and powerful from my clients. Simultaneously, I must retain my clinical judgment, skill and reserve so that I can deliver the best possible healing.

I guess I should tell you that I often cry with my clients too. I feel it's important to be an authentic human being. If I cry tears of compassion, that is a gift of myself and my heart to them. I am crying for them or with them; I don't leave them by letting my own life concerns dominate the foreground. It would be unreasonable to expect me to be unaware of my own life's issues.

Many therapists believe they have to remain aloof and objective and maintain a professional distance. In a moment of emotional intimacy, to me it seems inhumane not to extend my feelings for clients to them. I still am totally in my professional thinking, and my appropriate relationship, as provider, facilitator and teacher. My own agenda is not present in the foreground. It took me many years, and many lessons, to master the ability to emote and think at the same time, striking equilibrium between my empathetic self and professional perspective.

If the moment calls for it, I also touch or hold my clients. I believe it's the right thing to do. People need that tender, loving, healing touch. I do it in incremental steps, as I get to know the client and inquire about her comfort level. "Is it OK if I touch you or give you a hug or hold your hand?" I assess the moment. Will it distract her? Will it facilitate her to feel the experience more deeply? Or will it take her away from the experience? Sometimes, I'll get down on the floor with a client, and hold and rock her like a mother and child. People who have not had a loving paternal or maternal touch very much need it.

I want to touch clients on all levels: audibly, tactily, visually, emotionally, spiritually, intellectually and physically. I want the work to impact them on all these levels, and be thoroughly integrated throughout their organisms. Can you imagine that people who have been abused physically or sexually can experience love without touch? That physical contact must be offered at the pace that is right for the client, so I continually inquire.

Ideally in my work, original family members are included at some point in the process. When that is not possible, I have clients select individuals from the workshop to stand in for the people who are important to their story. I often find this much more powerful than using an empty chair, a common Gestalt technique in which people imagine someone sitting across from them. Having tangible human contact—skin, voice, heart and soul—enhances and intensifies the work. I am, however, watchful to design and monitor the action, so that no one else's personal projections color the experience.

Taking Responsibility

Each life contains joy and sorrow. As simple and obvious as this sounds, many of us have unrealistic expectations that life should have no pain or tragedy and that people should be without flaw and weakness. The victims of life are those who remain passive, carry resentment for the way their lives unfold, blame people for disappointing them, and avoid responsibility for the quality of their lives. They rage at the unfairness, refusing to accept that life is both fair and unfair.

The foundation of your work in life rests on taking responsibility for each moment, your actions and reactions, the quality of your relationships and the level of satisfaction you experience. When you take responsibility for your life, you become the artist, the creator of your own destiny. "My marriage isn't as fulfilling as I would like, and I'll take responsibility for that." "I want to find a better job, and I'll take responsibility for that." "I'm too alone, and I'll take responsibility for that." Try using the phrase, "and I'll take responsibility for that," without heaping guilt onto yourself. Taking responsibility empowers you.

Often people fight against this and want to remain the victims of misfortune, rather than developing the necessary life skills to create satisfaction. As a therapist, it's my job to have compassion for their pain, create exact moments of healing for their transformation, and simultaneously hold them accountable for their healing and their actualization of a healthier life.

I once read a piece of graffiti that said, "Take back responsibility for all your actions and reactions and you will free yourself from guilt and blame." Wisdom on the wall.

The most difficult cases are often those in which there has been violent abuse: sexual, physical or emotional. Even these people must step up to the plate, reconcile the past and move on so that they can create joy in their lives.

A woman had been physically abused throughout her childhood by her alcoholic mother. She developed into a deeply wounded, isolated, untrusting adult, who was unable to form lasting, loving relationships.

Her early work with me centered on getting her to the point where she moved through her anger and hurt to a place of forgiveness for her mother. She was a victim of long-term chronic trauma, and this process took 3 years. A powerful transformation occurred for this woman when her mother, who was alive and sober, in Alcoholics Anonymous, and most eager to make amends, consented to come to one of my workshops. She wanted to face head on what she had done to her daughter. With people in the workshop providing loving support for both the mother and daughter, the daughter spoke her truth to her mother.

The mother admitted that she had been drunk most of the time; there were many things she didn't remember. However, she allowed her daughter to recall for both of them the moments that had hurt her the most: the time she had burned her daughter on her back with a lighted cigarette, the multiple times she had hit her daughter with the full force of her hand, and the harsh and degrading things she had said to her daughter. The crescendo of this exact moment of healing for these women occurred when I asked the mother to lovingly and gently touch each part of her daughter's body that she had struck, and each time to sincerely apologize for the hurt, saying, "I'm so sorry I hurt you here. Please let me love you here now."

She started by gently lifting her daughter's hands, and carefully surrounding them with her own, saying, "I'm sorry I hurt you here. Please let me love you here now." Then she moved her hands to her daughter's face, "I'm sorry I hurt you here. Please let me love you here now." Then to the head, and the arms, and the back, and the thighs. The moment was so exquisite and intense, I found myself barely able to speak. The silence in the room seemed to uphold the sacredness of what was taking place.

It took every ounce of the daughter's strength and concentration to allow her mother to make physical and emotional contact with her in that way and to receive the gifts that were genuinely being offered. She could have lived a life of blame and fear and isolation; instead she chose to take responsibility, and do everything possible to heal her own wounds including inviting her mother to join her in the healing process. As her mother tearfully apologized with grace, her anguish, shame and sincerity were obvious.

In experiencing this moment, they both healed. The daughter was able to receive her mother, to let in the love and apologies she had needed for so long. The mother released her own tears, remorse and sorrow, and was given the precious opportunity to rewrite history and transform a tragedy into a triumph. The daughter ended up being rocked in her mother's arms while Pachabel's Canon in D Major soothed and supported them. The group slowly closed in around them, extending hearts and hands full of compassion and respect for the holiness that had just taken place.

Forgiveness

The experience of forgiveness is so powerful that it can bathe the entire nervous system and send a release of tension to every organ. It heals everyone who witnesses its reverent energy. Healing moments that touch you at this cellular level contain critical elements that respond to your organism's needs that have, up to now, not been met. For instance, when the daughter opened herself to the sacred act of forgiveness and allowed her mother to begin making amends, she purposefully moved beyond the trauma. She not only created a healing with her mother, but also sprouted within herself a new experience of mother and entered the process of reparenting, that is, becoming a good internal mother to herself.

New emotional wiring had been connected. Without a healing experience, there are no pathways to make a positive connection. Exact moments of healing, like the exchange of apology and forgiveness, begin from outside in, saturating the giver and the given on all levels like a heavy rain on dry ground, allowing growth to begin anew, facilitating health from inside out.

Rewriting History

A client in her mid-forties was still suffering from being molested as a 7-year-old child by a close and well-loved family friend. She kept this secret all her life, which made her feel like "damaged goods." This resulted in isolation, depression and mistrust of men and her own judgment.

After nearly a year of individual work with me, she felt ready to reveal her secret to her mother and father. Although her family was close and involved, they were emotionally unexpressive, especially her father. With my encouragement, she told them what had happened to her. They were shocked and devastated at her revelation. The friend was dead, so obviously no one could confront him with his betrayal.

When my client told her parents how important it was to her that they become involved in the process of healing this trauma, they were willing, yet frightened and even skeptical, which is typical and very understandable. I assured them that they had every right to be uncomfortable and concerned about the outcome and that I was committed to providing the very best for them and their daughter. I asked them to suspend judgment and trust me enough to try this. My experience had shown me that with the proper coaching, it would be a positive blessing for all.

They agreed to come to a weekend workshop. When it was time for my client to do her work, we set up the scene of the family's mountain vacation home, specifically the attic in which the friend had stayed and which was the location of the traumatic scene my client went through when she was just 7 years old. She had gone upstairs innocently and open-heartedly to see her friend and jump on his bed and wake him up. Instead, he was inebriated and pinned her to the floor and sexually abused her. She was shocked and terrified and blamed herself, a state that would remain as fixed unfinished business for more than three decades.

When asked what she would do differently if she had that opportunity, she said she wished she had screamed at the top of her lungs for her mom and dad to come running to her rescue and have their friend arrested. So that is exactly what we did. We simulated the scene the way it happened the first time. I always reconstruct the original traumatic scene as briefly as possible and just enough to stimulate memory. My heavy emphasis is always placed on the newly reconstructed scene, which provides the person with his or her ideal response to the original trauma.

I asked the men in the workshop who would be willing to act as the perpetrator. My client chose a middle-aged man, who was one of three men who volunteered, to sit in for what was acknowledged to be a difficult role. The initial reenactment of the events was brief with just enough intensity to awaken the memory and visually create the scene without retraumatizing the client.

Maintaining my professional objectivity during these moments is sometimes difficult, especially when I'm dealing with a client's memories of childhood abuse. My initial reaction can distract me with rage and judgment toward the perpetrator, especially when an innocent child has been so deeply wounded. Then I remember that, most likely, someone else had violated the perpetrator and that my job in the moment is to facilitate healing for the sake of everyone.

As the scene unfolded, the parents watched, visibly shaken and distraught at what had happened to their child at the hands of a man whom they had totally trusted. I instantly redesigned the moment, this time supporting and coaching the parents on how to rescue their daughter and provide absolutely everything that she had needed so long ago. As she finally released the screams for their help that had been lodged in her throat for so long, they ran bursting into the room. Her father was yelling at the top of his lungs to the perpetrator, "You son-of-a-bitch. I'm going to make you so sorry," as the mother, crying, dialed 911; the "simulated police" came and handcuffed the perpetrator and escorted him off to jail.

The daughter was then enveloped in the arms of her parents—sobbing and saying, "Help me, Daddy. Help me, Mommy," and they responded, "We're here, baby. You're all right now. We'll take care of you. We'll take care of everything. You didn't do anything wrong. We love you so much." For my client, this exact moment of healing helped her release years of pent-up emotion. Thinking she was sparing herself and her parents, the years of secretly carrying the horror had actually exacerbated the pain.

That moment clearly enabled her to express the enormity of her need and rewrite history, to speak the truth, and to be rescued and protected by her parents. As for her parents, this level of emotion was foreign to them, and yet I could see their hearts opening in front of my eyes as they embraced their daughter at a level of intimacy and truth they never knew was inside them. As they all sobbed and held one another, they were soothed by the music, Barbara Streisand singing the words, "No one is going to harm you, not while I'm around." The group of workshop participants softly closed in around them. There wasn't a person in the room left untouched by this experience.

Most people can't imagine having such healing moments; however, there is exaltation when they do. This is why I strongly encourage people to create them whether the significant other person is alive or dead, whether it's been a year or 50 years since the situation embedded itself into their consciousness. Timing to create an exact moment of healing is different for each person. Some may take a year or two in therapy before addressing serious trauma, especially if there is shame involved. Many people who come to work with me have already done years of recovery, and they're ready to co-create exact moments of healing.

Spontaneous Moments

Along with professionally designed moments of healing, there are also spontaneous moments of healing that arrive "out of the blue." The gracious hand of Providence unexpectedly reaches from some invisible realm and blesses you with a gift. Sometimes unsolicited, sometimes prayed for, these spontaneous exact moments of healing always respond to a need, and a solution shows up from a source outside yourself. Spontaneous moments are surprises that unexpectedly fall into your lap. They're perfect. Just what you needed in your life in the moment they happened. For instance, think back on a time when you were feeling anxious or confused about something in your life, and a person or situation appeared from "nowhere" to shed some light and support you in making the right decision. These surprising moments have the feeling of a blessing bestowed. I have heard it said that coincidences are sometimes God's way of remaining anonymous. Whether they are divine intervention, serendipity, accidents or the universe providing an exact moment of healing, they are a perfect response to a felt need. They leave us with a feeling of connectedness to powers greater than ourselves.

These coincidences, concurrences, and twists of fate can make your hair stand on end. Oh my God, I can't believe that just happened. They can "drop as gentle rain upon the place beneath," or they can arrive like a clap of thunder. I absolutely adore these moments. They connect me to the Grand Designer who sees all, knows all and can do all. I remember that I'm not alone, that anything is possible and that miracles are happening all the time. Most of all, I'm reminded that all of us are invisibly connected.

When I was 13 years old, I was a surprised recipient of some life-changing words. Weighing 160 pounds, and standing 5'2", I felt ugly and invisible. My girlfriend's Uncle Keanen turned to me one day, and said aloud for everyone to hear, "Look at her. She's beautiful. When she's 16, the boys are going to be lining up." Until then, with no father of my own, no grown man had ever verbally acknowledged my beauty. From that point onward, I saw a prettier face in the mirror. I received his comments as truth. There was hidden beauty in me, and I went on to lose 35 pounds and grow 6 inches by my 16th birthday. I gratefully remember that exact moment with Uncle Keanen as if it were yesterday. It had a profound effect on me and was what I now call an exact moment of healing.

In recalling this story, it was a bend in the road. I had a seriously overweight mother, who had enormous shame about her body. She used food as a substitute for love and comfort. She naturally proceeded to love me via food, instead of affection and contact (although I must admit I light up at the thought of another one of her pop-overs!) As a child, I complied with her introject that food is love, and assumed I was destined to have her body and be alone. Uncle Keanen provided a vision of myself in a new light, a possibility that I had never seriously considered. I remember waking up and shifting into a fierce determination to not live my mother's life and to be on my own path, which would include joy in my body and the ability for intimate connections.

I have experienced both spontaneous and professionally designed exact moments of healing around the same need.

My mother came from a privileged, Irish Catholic family who lived on Philadelphia's Main Line. The family was so devout that my grandmother received a personal telegram from the Pope on the morning she was married, sending her blessings. The family donated so much money to the archdiocese that they named Hallahan High School after the family. My mother was a bright, accomplished young woman who was an outstanding athlete, equestrian and national oratory champion, as well as a debutante. She went on to become successful as the first woman real estate broker on the Main Line. By the age of 20, she was also tragically alcoholic.

My father came from a line of strict Presbyterians; his grandfather and father were PhD theologians. My grandfather was a personal advisor to President Taft, and the chaplain of Syracuse University. Perhaps it was in part my father's rigid upbringing that drove him to become an alcoholic while a student at Syracuse.

He was a brilliant man and would go on to become the minister of supplies to Australia during World War II, and the manager of the first and now defunct Yankees "football" team in New York.

My parents married, each for the first time, later in life. They met when my mother was 36 and my father 38. Following a 3-week alcoholic binge, they became engaged. Because my father was not Catholic, the church considered it a mixed marriage not worthy of a sacrament and would not allow my mother and father to be married in the main sacristy. My father's family was not happy to be under any Catholic roof, let alone the side altar of the church. This was only the beginning of an impossible pairing of two well-intentioned, unhealthy individuals.

Two years into this actively alcoholic marriage, I was born. Having a child did not stop my parents from drinking and fighting. One morning, after a hurtful drinking episode, my mother arranged for one of her friends to escort my father to a train bound for New York and told him never to return to Pennsylvania. He pleaded with my mother to let him return to help raise his daughter. I was only 2 1/2 at the time. My mother held her ground. In response, my father hired a lawyer. It made little difference because this was a time when the courts didn't honor the rights of fathers. In the end, my father told my mother that if she didn't allow him to rejoin the family, we would never see him again. That suited her perfectly.

I never saw my father again, and my mother rarely mentioned him. When she did, it would be with disdain or a comment like, "You can't get blood from a rock." She did grant him his brilliant mind, and would say that he was handsome and distinguished, and wore an ascot "like the man in the Calvert Whiskey ad."

Even with these snippets of information, I still spent my entire childhood and adolescence fantasizing about what it would be like to meet my father. What would I say to him? What would he do? Why did he leave me? Did he know who I was? Did he think about me? Was he looking for me in crowds as I was looking for him? Would I shake his hand and say, "Hello Mr. Fenton" with prideful distance and formality, or would I break down in tears and throw my arms around him saying the never spoken word—Daddy?

I prayed hard for just one moment to be with my father. It never happened. When I was 20 years old, in a rare moment of physical contact, my mother put her arm around my shoulder and announced, "Honey, your Daddy died." In a state of shock, not comprehending the word *Daddy* because it had never been used in my presence, the thought went through me, "Daddy, who's Daddy?"

It was arranged by his sister, my Aunt Kay, that her son, Phil, would drive to New York City to claim my father's body at the city morgue. However, en route, Phil's car broke down and my Aunt Kay called my mother to report what was happening. I overheard the quandary about what to do next and, without thinking, I said, "I'm going." My boyfriend, Rick, insisted on driving me. I left my mother sitting drunk in her chair and headed for New York City to find my father.

When we arrived in New York, Rick suggested I not go to the morgue. He felt that having only one visual memory of my father dead on a slab would be continually traumatizing for me. It would be better to find someone who knew him to identify the body. We decided to pick up my cousin, Baba, who lived in New York, to help with the search. I called home for my father's address.

My father, it turned out, lived on the Upper East Side of Manhattan. This was another shock. My mother had always told me he was a bum living in the Bowery, a section of New York, which, at that time, was noted for it's preponderance of homeless, alcoholic, drug addicted, ne'er-do-well lost souls. Now I heard he was a resident of an upscale, brownstone apartment house. I was disoriented and bewildered.

Feeling small and vulnerable, I tentatively walked up the seemingly massive five steps to the entrance and rang the bell beside the large wooden doors. The landlord answered, and after I introduced myself, he told me how my father had been sick, and had vomited all over the stairway several nights earlier. He would show me to his apartment, a third floor walk-up. It was a climb I would remember all the days of my life.

The stairway was dark with little to no natural light. Each floor had two wide sets of twelve steps angled back and forth. The steps themselves were old, wooden and worn. I was barely breathing. Scared. What am I going to find? Could this be real? How bad is it going to hurt? The sound of each step echoed the beat of my heart. I was for the first time placing my feet where my father had placed his. Each new step intensified my anguish and fear and yet I had to walk on. I had to know. I had to meet him in whatever way I could. Who was he? Was there any shred of connection? Did I really ever have a father? Did I even have a right to be here? With each step another question arose. Another rush of pain. The climb felt endless.

The landlord had boarded up the apartment after my father's body was removed. Two eight foot two-by-fours created an "X" over the door. It felt like a crime scene. Although the hallway was hot, my body was in a cold sweat. I was trembling inside and dazed. As the landlord pried off the wooden "X" and opened the door, an overwhelming putrid stink of death hit me in the face. The stench made me initially step back and turn my head. It would linger with me for weeks afterwards. Early July had been very hot and my father had been dead in the apartment at least 2 or 3 days before anyone found him.

At this point, I felt as though I had entered the Twilight Zone. Could this really be happening? Am I really here? After all the years of wondering where he was, I was now where he lived, breathed, and ate and where he called home.

The apartment opened into a large living room with an old

oriental rug, couch and television. Puddles of dried blood on the rug and floor stunned me further. What happened? Why is there blood? Did he kill himself? Did he drink himself to death? Would there be blood if he had a heart attack? Loaded with thoughts and questions, I voiced nothing. I was only 20 years old, feeling more like 6, and I had no answers. I walked on.

His bedroom was to the rear left of the living room. It was a simple room with a double bed, two night tables and a chest of drawers. When I slowly opened the top bureau drawer, I felt breathless, as though I were going to faint. There, in the middle of the drawer, was his watch, a gold wedding ring and a Mason's ring. And neatly placed in the lower left-hand corner, were photographs of me, his only child, from the time I was a baby. He even had an envelope marked "Mariah's first haircut" with the bright red locks still tucked inside. I picked up the largest photograph, my high school senior portrait, which I've put on the cover of this book, and stared at it. I was stunned. In my awareness, he had not seen an image of me since he left when I was 2 1/2. I stood there, frozen for the longest time staring at that picture in my hand. I couldn't move. I felt my legs would buckle if I took a step. I had no language. No words. I was filled with "I have a father." In that moment, I had this clear, overwhelming knowing that the man who supposedly didn't want to remember that I was born, had been living with the same silent longing to see me as I had to see him. I cried.

To this day, I don't really know how he died. There was no autopsy. Everyone assumed that his death was alcohol induced. Nevertheless, there I was in the home of the most important man I never knew. I learned later that his sister, my aunt Kay, had been sending him photographs and updates of me throughout my life.

With the landlord's help, I did find someone at his favorite haunt, the Shamrock Café, to identify the body at the morgue. I was in no shape for more trauma. I found a funeral home across the street from the café and arranged a memorial service for my father that included a receiving line. While Baba attended to my inebriated mother in a back room, I stood alone on the line and shook hands one by one with all my father's friends and acquaintances. The Shamrock Café had closed for the hours of the service so that everyone could attend. It was painful to discover that most of them didn't even know he had a daughter. His closest friend, the one who had identified the body, did know and confided that just prior to his death, my father shared his desire to be reunited with me and to take me on a special trip to Europe.

Hearing this information and seeing my photographs and locks of hair in his dresser drawer totally shifted my identity from a rejected daughter to a treasured, lost child. For the first time in my memory, I knew my father loved me. This was a profound spontaneous exact moment of healing. I would never again be as I was even five minutes earlier.

It's one thing to have these moments and another to create alchemy for yourself. As I mentioned in the previous chapter, positively integrating these healing moments into our souls, our being, is the crucial labor of sustaining personal health.

This integration also clears a path for new positive experiences. As I integrated finding my pictures and locks of my hair in my father's dresser after his death, I shifted from living with the chronic agonizing pain of abandonment to a woman loved by my father. As miraculous as that transformation was, it also became a catalyst for integrating even deeper levels of his love. I became open to men more capable of mature love than I had chosen in the past, which paved the way for marriage and motherhood. When my children were the same age I was when I lost my father, I knew first hand the intense bond and love between a parent and child, and could imagine how devastated he must have been when he lost me. So the integration of that first moment of discovering his love continues at deeper and deeper levels, enriching my life and making me more whole.

Over time I was also able to filter out the painful parts of walking into my father's apartment; the stench, the blood, my pain. And I was able to selectively contain what was precious about it in what I call my "forever place," a spot in my body tucked softly behind my heart. That filtering allowed me to eliminate what was toxic, and to digest and assimilate what was nourishing about the whole experience.

To this day, I have had many moments of deep gratitude and self-change because of this experience, and continue to integrate the healing impact of that moment. Integration of healing moments begets new healing moments to be integrated. Integration makes your experience part of your personal fiber. When you integrate a healing moment, you make it your own. You become it. The more healing moments you integrate, the healthier you become. When you integrate a gift well, you are momentarily and forever changed.

It wasn't until several years later, when I attended my first psychotherapy workshop as a student, that I experienced the power of a professionally designed exact moment of healing. After I told the group the story about my father, the leader asked me to choose someone in the group to comfort me. Not realizing what I was doing, I co-created my own exact moment of healing by choosing a white-haired man in his sixties, who I later learned was Father John, a Roman Catholic priest who had come to the workshop to learn how to positively influence one person's life. He had been frustrated by the constant ministering to large groups.

The moment in the workshop that had the most impact for me was when the group leader asked Father John to hold me and rock me in his arms while the rest of the group sang "Sunrise, Sunset." I know my father had held me as an infant, but I had no sense of it until this moment. In Father John's arms, I felt totally transported back to when I was a baby. I surrendered to the unmistakable physical infusion of his love. It was literally the first time that an older man had ever held me since my father left home. In a combination of profound relief and anguish, I sobbed and finally uttered the precious word, "Daddy." The meeting with my father that I had fantasized over and over, year after year, had in this most unusual way arrived. I had had my reunion in the form of a precious "exact moment of healing." I will carry its sweetness for the rest of my life. Even today when I hear or read stories about a child being reunited with a parent, I well up with tears.

The experience of abandonment and rejection from my own life, and from what I have learned as a therapist, has made me keenly aware that many of my clients live lives driven by this kind of unfinished business that needs to be healed. Certain memories stick in your system and strongly color—positively or negatively, consciously or unconsciously—your actions, decisions and emotional reactions to life's events. It is important that your current life not be controlled by the past.

Pay close attention to possibilities that present themselves as an invitation or an opening to Divine intervention, which can happen in a string of events. My cousin's car breaking down opened a door for me to walk through. Had I not walked through, I would have missed the perfect moment of healing that happened when I opened my father's drawer and discovered the love I so desperately needed.

Receive the Gifts

Spontaneously occurring exact moments of healing can drop like a gift from the heavens. We've all had them. Moments happen and they feel magical and mystical, and they respond to an unmet need you are having. Recognize possibilities for healing when they're presented to you. Wish for them, be ready for them, be open for them; they can happen anytime, anyplace, around the bend, out of the blue.

Receive the gifts. Inhale and let them saturate your being. Celebrate them. Be grateful. Absorb the feeling. Shout or whisper a prayer of thanks, and rest in the knowing that you are heard.

Self-Directed Moments

Mark Nepo, in his brilliant and inspiring book, *The Exquisite Risk*, wrote about the power of directing your life, "It is the drifting and steering along the way, and the turning of experience into that which keeps us alive—this is the necessary art from which we live and breathe. It is how we find our way."

Self-created exact moments of healing are moments you bravely design and implement on your own with the purpose and intention to heal a wound, fill a hole, finish old business, risk more aliveness or breathe life into a dream. Often, they require artistry and care, for they are sensitive and unpracticed actions or exchanges. They release you into metamorphosis—shedding of old skin to reveal the new. Only with skill, creativity and courage can you create a force strong enough to ensure you find your way.

It is from the deep knowing of yourself that you can discover these missing and necessary moments in your life that you need to create, the ones that can unlock your paralysis and stop repetition of old erosive patterns.

As with every new step, you're likely to feel apprehensive,

even fragile. You'll need your breath, your undivided support and your promise to be the first one there to pick yourself up if you fall flat on your face.

These moments can also be simple and sweet, like feeling alive and brand new after jumping off a diving board for the first time. These little risks exercise your capacity to create change, and can bring sunshine to an otherwise dreary day or dreary existence.

For example, I grew up knowing nothing of men. I lost my father very early in life, had no brothers and went to an all girls' private Catholic school. I knew this deficit could affect my quality of life and needed my attention. So I spent a number of years learning about men; purposely befriending them, spending time with them and inquiring about them. I let men know I needed fathering, brothering and male friendship. I also spent a lot of time fathering myself, imagining myself as my ideal father talking to me, taking me to the zoo and flying me high on the swings. I got really creative in reparenting myself, providing for all those unmet needs. Each time, I was creating my own exact moments of healing and transforming my experience of being an abandoned child to a well-loved child. I should add that it was important that I believed my own father would have loved to have provided these moments for me and that he would be fully in support of my standing in for him, giving me what he could not.

You are the artist of every day, hour, minute, second. Empower yourself with the knowledge that you always have choice. All of your life you choose, whether it's simply what to wear and eat, where to live and work, what friends to cultivate, what places to go. When something negative happens, you have the choice of asking, "Why me?" which is the victim's role or taking the healthier approach of "This is what is, how do I want to deal with it?" Realization of choice and your healthy implementation of it moves you from victim to victor, from passive to active, from "I have to" to "I choose to," from wounded adult child to responsible adult. In reaching this point in your personal development, you cross a threshold of transformation.

What sweet small moment could you choose to create in your life today that would stretch your capacity to make creative contact with yourself, others and the world and would somehow reflect a need or want? Could you greet your spouse in a new way that would align more perfectly with your desire to hone your skills of loving communication? That simple step requires awareness of your desire for personal growth, willingness to claim self-responsibility and power to choose and take skillfully designed action. If you repeat the behavior often enough it will sink under your skin, and eventually become who you are without you having to think about it.

What's important is this; you are in this lifetime only once. You are charged with the responsibility for knowing, treasuring and providing for this being—you. If you want to excel and grow yourself into the person you have the potential to be, you must have a high level of awareness and a willingness to face and provide for the ever-present needs of your organism. In one form or another, you will need your own skill in creating exact moments of healing. You'll also need the ability to discern whether you would benefit most from professional assistance or by creating a moment independently.

When I was in my early twenties and had just begun seeing a therapist, I decided to take my mother out for dinner and ask her to tell me everything she remembered about my father. I was prepared to do it in a skillful way, telling her how much it would mean to me if she could stretch beyond what was comfortable to her and give this gift of information. I was determined to not let her deflect, dodge the point or solely disparage my father.

While we were eating, I noticed a man, very properly attired in a handsome suit and tie, sitting alone and seemingly aware of our conversation. I did not feel intruded upon; in fact, I felt distinct support coming my way. I wondered about him. Did he have a daughter? What was so interesting to him about our conversation? He was clearly keeping me company and I felt protected.

The conversation with my mother went very well. I told her how important it was to know more about my father and that I recognized it was painful and difficult for her to speak about him. She sincerely tried to recall facts about my father. In doing so, she admitted he wasn't all bad. He could be a charming and engaging conversationalist, loved fly-fishing, was very dapper, and liked to wear ascots. She told me he was protective of me and would have kept me in a glass cage where no one could hurt me. She even volunteered that if she had to do it all over again, she would have gotten them both help for their alcoholism.

Her admissions of his value brought deep sighs of relief. I had needed her positive acknowledgement of him for a long time. Prior to this conversation, she had only given me the image of him as a drunken bum in New York's bowery, a lie I had believed, to the day he died, as truth.

As important as some of the details about my father were, it was equally important that I asserted my right to speak of him, and claim him as my father. She had trained me to always tell people that she was my mother and father, as if I had suffered no loss. I was no longer willing to do that for her.

As we were leaving the restaurant, the gentleman also got up and held the door for us. Walking past him, I felt shy. When he looked me straight in the eyes and nodded affirmatively, I felt grateful. His acknowledgment and support went directly to my heart. Although I have no idea who he was, he felt like a gift of a father's presence and support. It was an enormous relief. I had created a critically important exact moment of healing for myself that was blessed with a complement of a spontaneous moment of healing, a gift of assistance in my moment of need.

Breakthrough Moments

Diane, one of my clients, after ending her marriage to an emotionally unhealthy man, felt totally devastated and dependent. She could not imagine surviving alone. Since her divorce she had worked hard to increase her self-love and acceptance, and had become independent, both financially and emotionally. She had also developed a community of supportive friends. Nonetheless, after all this work, she continued to choose unsafe and unhealthy men, desperate for them to rescue her. This pattern had brought a lot of pain into her life.

While watching other women deal with relationships at a recent workshop, it became crystal clear to her that she desired a life partner, even marriage. She told me she didn't go to the workshop to look for a man (as she had some years); she went for herself. Although currently in a relationship, Diane knew it did not support her emotionally and would not result in a long-term commitment. The work she witnessed clarified for her that life's challenges are more easily met if partnered with a healthy person who can provide a safe, soft place to land and a shoulder to lean on. She realized that what she needed most was a safe person who accepted all of her just as she is and who would go deeper with her and commit to her.

With this new-found clarity and strength, Diane decided to create her own exact moment of healing with her boyfriend in which each could express honest feelings and needs. This wasn't easy; it was a new behavior for her to be so direct and supportive of her own needs. She told him she needed more love and affection, open and honest communication and monogamy. This self-supporting and direct communication enabled him to be more truthful about his inability to meet her needs, and to commit to the relationship. Although they ended their relationship, she currently feels hope for new possibilities. She had created a breakthrough moment of healing for herself that brought with it a new kind of excitement. She now feels like she can trust herself, that she's in her own good hands, safe and protected, this time by herself. Diane finally feels ready and more equipped for a healthy relationship that comes from love of self, and not from old unmet needs.

Self-directed moments of healing can be created at any time and at any place. The key is knowing what you need to heal and which old wounds are negatively impacting your life. If you know you need to trust, or you know you need to change your damaged view of men, an occasion of healing often presents itself. And it's your awareness of what you need that allows you to pick up on it. Look for trust. Look for and study good relationships around you. Look for and spend time with good men in the world, as opposed to untrustworthy men who reinforce your old wounds. Purposefully validate a new reality and integrate a new perspective in order to undo an old introject. Remember, introjects are beliefs you have swallowed whole, some of which limit and contaminate your life.

If you think there's no kindness in the world, look around when you're in a supermarket, or a business meeting and notice kindness. Tell yourself, look, there it is, a kind person behaving in kind ways. Here's a person I can trust, or a person who won't hurt me. Make contact with that person. Just say hello. As a disabled person, I often tell my friends to come with me for a day and see another part of life, a display of human kindness. So look all around you for antidotes to your dysfunctional convictions, and for opportunities to experience life in new enriching ways.

I have a client who took advantage of being in what I call an *occasion of healing*. While with his children on a day trip to the museum at Ellis Island in New York, he was emotionally overcome by the photographs on the walls of immigrants coming into this country. Like them, he was never sure at any given moment if he would be accepted, and always lived in fear of rejection.

By age 10, despair and anguish had engulfed him due to the early death of his mother and the shame and embarrassment caused by his alcoholic, philandering father. Forced to lie in order to maintain his father's secrets, he could never truly be himself in the world. He felt like unwanted, contaminated goods, as if his father's shame was his own.

At the museum, across from the entrance, are the stations where immigration officers interviewed immigrants. Beyond those stations was a stairway, divided into three sections. The first stairway was for those who passed through and were accepted into the United States, destined for New York City. The second stairway is for those who were accepted and headed to the ticket office to arrange transit to other parts of the country. The third stairway is for those who were being denied, quarantined or arrested.

As he sat looking in the eyes of all the souls in the photographs on the walls, seeing their tension and imagining what it was like for them, it dawned on him that he could use this opportunity to create an exact moment of healing. He knew he needed to feel like he belonged.

So he stood up, took a deep breath, and looked around to take in the environment. Then he purposefully walked up to the podium with his head held high. He made a conscious point of not feeling intimidated, of not acting like he was holding and hiding the family secret with which he had been raised. He had to let that go and feel accepted.

At the podium, he gave a little speech in his mind about how he was a good person with a good heart, who had done nothing wrong and who deserved and was entitled to be accepted. Then he took another deep breath, and walked down the steps of acceptance. He made a point of feeling and experiencing each footstep. As he descended, he began to feel a sense of exuberance and joy, accompanied by a powerful sense of relief. That was when he became aware of the tension he had been carrying in his muscles because that tension began to release and he was able to replace that energy with a sense of peace.

When he got to the bottom of the steps, he experienced a subtle yet distinct shift in his self-esteem, and was delighted in his conscious decision to have created this moment, for carrying it out, and for recognizing that it was another step in the process of healing.

As a by-product of creating this moment of healing, he reported that whenever he sees an image of the Statue of Liberty (which is surprisingly often), he's reminded of that day and he remembers the impact of the choice he made. His self-directed exact moment of healing offered a therapeutic response to one pressing need within his configuration of needs about his traumatic family history. And every time he recalls that moment, it is another moment of healing, adding to the cumulative effect of healing moments, permanently altering the original pain and trauma.

There will be many moments that you need or you simply want to have that you can create on your own. You have learned about healthy living, the constant cycling around of becoming aware, feeling your feelings, defining and meeting your needs both simple and large as they emerge, giving and receiving provisions, then cycling again.

There are many longings you can respond to on your own by purposefully creating experiences that meet the call of these unmet needs. Apologize to a friend. Express your pain or resentment to someone who hurt you. Create a meaningful memorial service for someone whom you have not thoroughly mourned. Have that conversation you've been too afraid to have. Express a deeper more vulnerable need to a spouse. Spend time around a friend's healthy marriage so that you can learn about wholesome interdependency. Forgive someone for whom you've held resentment for too long. The possibilities are endless. What's important is that you take action that precisely responds to what your organism needs to achieve balance or homeostasis. These moments of healing can lift you out of your stuckness; free you up to grow beyond old repetitive patterns, compulsions and barriers, and empower you to chart a new course. They are a relief to the heart and soul.

The Healing Journey

It's hard to replicate on paper the poignancy and power of these healing moments. Although intangible, they penetrate the organism at an energetic level deep below the surface that often goes beyond words or even practical understanding. Healing moments are both fleeting and eternal. Their immediate and long-term results are measurable and profound.

In this book I have described the healing spirit and theory of creating exact moments of healing. I also have shared some basic principles of heart and soul-based Gestalt theory so that you can more fully understand how it works and why I do what I do with each client. This book is not meant to be an in-depth theoretical presentation. Rather it's written to touch your heart and inspire you to consider your own life and the potential for creating your own exact moments of healing. Whether you need to face contaminating unfinished business from your past, address a present life crisis, or manifest your dreams, it is my hope that you will gain insight into your issues and find the courage to provide for yourself all that your heart needs to fully heal and become the person you want to be. My wish is that the following chapters and stories of healing and redemption will serve as bright stars to illuminate your journey.

Tales of a Wounded Healer

It takes courage to grow up and become who you really are.

—ee cummings

Chapter Five

MACK—WELCOME HOME JOURNEY

"Helicopters dropped us off in the jungle and didn't come back to get us for 2 weeks, once for 2 months—one time we were out for 7 months. One military operation after the next kept us in the jungle. At night we slept in holes we dug for ourselves at each campsite.

"Back then I was scared all the time. But you weren't allowed to express it. I was a Marine. In the Marines it's not cool to say you're scared. I wasn't so much afraid of dying as I was of the firefights. And the hand-to-hand combat didn't bother me as much as the booby traps. The Vietcong were big on that. I saw lots of guys step on landmines and get their legs blown off. Others were blown into so many pieces there wasn't a fucking thing to send home."

I met Mack for the first time when he applied for admission to our 3-year training program. He arrived early for our appointment, and was patiently sitting in the waiting room when I entered. As we shook hands, I noticed that he was a ruggedly handsome man with a Mediterranean complexion—dark brown hair and watchful brown eyes. He was immaculately dressed in casual clothes. I guessed him to be in his early to mid-forties.

During our interview, he told me he had been in Vietnam as a marine for three consecutive tours of duty between 1966 and 1972 and that the war trauma he experienced had led him into drug and alcohol addiction for more than a decade. The man now sitting in front of me, however, had been in addiction recovery for many years, had earned a college degree, had gotten married and had two children, and had undergone extensive psychotherapy.

Mack's vast life experience distinguished him from our usual training program candidates. Although he had grown apart, in many ways, from the tough working-class neighborhood where he had been raised, his background often revealed itself through his street-savvy language and expressions. Another remnant of his rough life was his name, M-A-C-K, tattooed one letter on each finger. I imagined this served as a personalized roadmap that had saved him from losing himself along the way. This was a man whose face and eyes carried the sorrow and wisdom of someone who had seen too much for any one lifetime.

Speaking directly and passionately, he told me that he wanted to get into our program; he knew beyond a shadow of a doubt that he wanted to be a therapist, and he wanted me to train him. With this strong purposeful energy and apparent natural intelligence, Mack impressed me as a man with a mission and the perseverance to ensure his success. He had the fierce determination of a warrior who was ready to do whatever was required to win and appeared unafraid of the work that lay ahead of him.

We accepted Mack into the training program, which involves extensive theoretical and experiential instruction along with clinical supervision. It also requires students to explore important issues in their own lives that are in need of healing. I knew from the start that Mack would have to do deep personal work on his Vietnam experiences. In many ways it was still his master. We needed to heal the wounds so that Vietnam could become part of his past and, hopefully, a springboard from which he could do great things in the future. The timing of his "Vietnam work," however, would have to come from Mack. I place a great deal of trust in the process and in the student, and expect my students to set the pace and lead the way. They do.

For Mack, it took time for him to feel comfortable and to trust both my skill and the good intentions of the group. It wasn't until the end of his first year in the program, at a weekend training, that he experienced his first "exact moment of healing."

At that time, all of our local trainings and workshops were held at an old mansion on the grounds of the Daylesford Abbey, a Norbertine religious community in Paoli, Pennsylvania. The building, called *Pinebrook*, contained a large open room, probably a large living room at one time, and a whole wall of windows centered around a set of French doors overlooking a beautiful garden and open fields. The room itself was warm and comfortable and students mostly sat on pillows or beach chairs. The building had a history, and a feeling of spiritual purpose mingled with a touch of homelike familiarity. After all, Pinebrook, in one of its lives, once housed seminarians hoping to become Norbertines. The environment was nurturing and supportive of my work. I imagined all those prayers and chants were embedded deep into the wood, brick and mortar, blessing us all.

Our usual design at training weekends is for me to coach a student therapist while he or she works with a student client. It intrigued me that Mack volunteered to be the client and selected Irene as his therapist. Irene was a 75-year-old social worker, with a loving presence, who had recently lost most of her eyesight to disease. Perhaps Mack saw in her a fellow comrade who also had suffered great losses in the trenches of life and who now carried her own battle wounds with grace and dignity, while maintaining an open-heartedness.

There were about 20 students in Mack's class, plus myself and two other trainers, Dori Middleman and Mark Putnam, both psychiatrists who work primarily from a Gestalt approach. Usually, the class sits in a circle, with an empty chair serving as an "open" seat for whichever student is ready to do personal work. When Mack took the seat at the head of the circle, it was clear that he was anxious. His hands trembled and there was a slight sheen on his forehead from sweat. The group sensed his discomfort and recognized that this was a critical opening for Mack. We all sat quietly and with full attention as he continued sharing his wartime memories.

"I remember this one guy. I can't remember his name or face but I remember he was young. He was standing beside a haystack, and he kept sticking his head out to look. I kept telling him to get the fuck down. I said that about two or three times and then I kind of looked away and I heard a round zing and I heard the thump. As soon as I heard that, I knew he was hit. He got it right between the eyes. He looked like a rubber doll falling down. I remember going crazy. I started jumping on top of him and shaking him screaming—'Why the hell didn't you get the fuck down.'

"To the Vietcong, to fight and die for your country meant that the battle wasn't over until the last guy was dead. To this day, I'm not sure how I survived. I saw a lot of my friends die. My company had 365 guys. In the end, me and another guy were the only ones alive."

As I looked around the room, I saw that everyone was deeply moved by Mack's story. Some people were crying; some were holding one another. Not only did we each have our own feelings of guilt, loss and anger at that war, but now we had opened ourselves to Mack's personal experience. We couldn't help but identify with him, each in our own way. A group's willingness to openly embrace the pain of each individual moves that person out of isolation into a collective carrying of the pain. This alchemy occurred in our group, where we readily shifted Mack's pain into our pain. An organic upswell of healing energy from the group was immediately directed toward Mack.

I could feel my heart racing and tears welling up as Mack's images of his wartime hell flooded my mind. It was excruciating to imagine this beautiful 18-year-old boy experiencing such horror. For a moment, I felt a panic rush through me. I thought of my own two sons, Luke and Cole, and the possibility of their being called to war and experiencing a friend get a bullet between his eyes or worse—coming home in a body bag themselves.

I also remembered the daily ritual of watching the news with my mother, and listening to reports of how many young men died each day in Vietnam. I remember calling my neighbor, Jay, and other male friends, to see what number they had in the draft lottery. In that war, all males at 18 years of age were given a lottery number. The lower the number, the sooner you were called. I had also worried about my cousin, Charlie, who was in Vietnam. Even though he was no in a combat position because of a leg injury from childhood, he was still in harm's way in a war where anything could happen.

I thought of my high school boyfriend, Danny, who had told me he didn't think he would live to see his twenty-first birthday. He didn't. He died at age twenty of shrapnel wounds in Vietnam; his father had died in the Korean War. I still remember his funeral, seeing his only remaining brother—now, too, in a Marine's uniform.

He had signed up when he heard Danny had been killed. Then the look on his mother's face—empty and hollow, and the playing of taps. My body shook each time the honor guards fired their rifles into the gray sky, and I cried into my mother's shoulder.

All of these memories flew by in a matter of seconds! And I knew others in the room were having their own flashbacks of the war. That's when I caught sight of Tim, another trainee whom I knew had been a conscientious objector during the Vietnam War. He hid in Canada and waged his own war with America's military policies. Mack's story and Tim's, although appearing very different, actually paralleled one another in many ways. Tim, too, had buried his anger and fear in drug addiction and petty crime. And he wasn't safely home yet either. I didn't know how much the two men had shared outside the workshop. At this moment, however, Tim was sitting with his head in his hands, tears streaming down his face, clearly affected by what was happening.

"There was a guy in my unit. He came over 3 or 4 months after me. He got shot in the neck—blood pouring out. They couldn't get a medivac wagon to him. He and a medic were pinned down. I got fuckin' pissed, and I said I'm going to get him. My intention was to strap him on my back and crawl back with him. The guys kept saying to me don't go, you're fuckin' crazy, you're gonna get zapped. But I had to go. I took off my flak jacket (that protects you from shrapnel), my ammo and my helmet and I ran about 30 yards to where they were. The corpsman had shot him up with morphine. I remember talking with them, but I can't remember what we said. They called in an artillery round that put up a smokescreen so that the medivac wagon could get in there. We got him on that, and we got out of there. I had to do that.

"Man, by the end of my third tour in Vietnam, I thought about suicide a lot—how easy it would be. When I got on the plane to go home, I felt so fucking old. But I was only 23. My head was telling me that I was relieved to get out of this hellhole, but man, my heart was telling me I felt sad and guilty that I was still alive. When I got home, I got my

first look at how the country had changed. Instead of people saying thanks to us, we were getting spit on by these longhaired hippies."

Here before me was a beautiful man who had indeed survived, and who was still raw and unmended after twenty years. I felt the critical nature of the job at hand and the awesome responsibility to discover what he needed to heal. At that moment, I prayed for guidance.

In this piece of work, since it was so clinically important, I chose to give more direction than usual in my supervision. And Irene, the student therapist, had asked for my help. She did everything I told her to do. My belief is that as a therapist, you can take your clients only as far as you've gone yourself. Before Mack could function professionally as a therapist, at the level he desired, he had an enormous amount of healing to do. He had witnessed the tragic and gruesome deaths of comrades and had to repeatedly swallow his true reactions to save his own life. These memories ate him up inside. His "unfinished business" around Vietnam had been a major contributor to his drug and alcohol addiction, and other self-destructive behaviors.

To digest and integrate the Vietnam memories that traumatized him all these years, I knew Mack had to revisit his Vietnam memories. He had to identify what remained unfinished, and what needs were still unmet from that time. I needed to do just enough to stimulate a body memory, but not too much, so as to avoid retraumatizing him. I could then respond and provide his organism with what it needed to heal. Obviously, I couldn't bring back his comrades but, by coaching him and the other trainees through a simulation, I could uncover some of his most repressed and damaging emotions and respond to them with therapeutic additions and healing interaction.

This process is very important for people such as Mack, who are suffering from post-traumatic stress disorders. Essentially, I simulate just enough of the original event to provide an experience of being there now, without triggering a traumatic response. My major emphasis is always on the corrective moment, the healing moment. I then clarify and provide what the person still needs to ensure satisfaction and completion. This experiential approach of creating an exact moment of healing that identifies and meets the unmet needs of the client is often profoundly effective. The wounds were acquired by experience and must be met and healed by experience.

As Mack continued immersing himself in this piece of work that brought him back to Vietnam, I knew he would discover specific unmet needs crying out for satisfaction. I also felt certain that the acknowledgment and appreciation that had organically arisen in the group for him, and for what he had done for us, would play a critical role in his healing. He had not fully realized this need and the real possibility of fulfillment, yet this was precisely what he needed and had never gotten.

"From 1970, when I was discharged from the army, to about 1984, my memory is a blur. During that time I got married, had two sons, acquired a criminal record and a list of minimum-wage jobs. I was also borderline psychotic, drinking heavily, and mixing two and three types of drugs. I didn't sleep much, but, when I did, I had violent, recurring dreams of Vietnam. I began to sleep with a gun. My paranoia made me fearful that Vietcong would come into my house and kill my family and me while we slept.

"It was a Friday night. I'd been drinking and drugging since seven that morning. It was a summer night; the full leaves of the trees reflected the light from the Minute Market across the street. To me, it created this mysterious aura. I was so messed up in my head that I began to fantasize I was back in Vietnam. For years, the neighborhood complained about the teenagers who hung out at the market. They destroyed property and went around peeking into peoples' windows at night. So I decided to do my Rambo thing. I got my guns and sneaked down a couple of houses closer to the market. In my distorted thinking, the teenagers were the Vietcong. As one of them approached close to where I was hiding, I jumped out and put a gun to his head, screaming that I was going to kill him. The kid was begging for his life. Something made me stop, and I ran away. The cops came

*by my house to question me, but they couldn't prove it was
me."*

It was clear that combat for Mack continued long after the war
ended. At this juncture of his story, I was thinking it seemed
miraculous that he was still alive, and that surely there must be a
meaningful purpose to his existence. If I could harness the survival
power that he possessed, and steer him fully away from self-
destructive behavior using that same enormous force for positive
self-support, there would be no limit to what he could do with his
life.

To give Mack what he most needed, I intently watched and
listened to him. I observed how he held his body. I listened to his
tone of voice and speech patterns. What fascinated me about him
was the difference between his written and spoken language. His
written work for the training program was sophisticated and
thoughtful using correct vocabulary and grammatical structure.
However, when he spoke about his boyhood in the streets at home,
or his time in the jungles of Vietnam, Mack talked like a tough guy.
He used inaccurate grammar, and liberally sprinkled his recollections
with curse words, particularly the word *fuck*. This was obviously a
survival tactic that he automatically carried over from youth and
certainly from Vietnam. It was clear to me that Mack had realized
back then on some psychic level, that softness or sadness could kill
him. Trust and emotional need could kill him. His life had literally
depended on that macho persona.

As I worked with Mack over the years, and became familiar
with the various aspects of his personality, I also sensed that there
were tender, loving parts of him that had been "buried alive," and
were longing to be released. These polarities that existed in Mack
exist in all of us, whether we are willing to own them or not. We are
composed of a wide range of qualities, characteristics and polarities.
To attain wholeness, we must become fully aware and take
responsibility for all of who we are—the best and the worst. Our
lovingness, our hatefulness, our generosity, our selfishness—all are
pieces of the whole. Only when we know who we are can we manage
ourselves and choose responsible behavior.

When people own up to only one side of a polarity, they are
not equipped for healthy relationships. They truly do not know

who they are and will defend against the awareness of their more unattractive characteristics. They will deny to themselves and others how cold, critical and selfish they can be and insist that they are always warm, kind and generous. This blinds them to their own contribution to problems and their lack of commitment to working on resolution.

To be a healthier person, it's imperative that you own and have compassion for the negative and positive sides of yourself. When you own your negative characteristics, it's not for the purpose of saying "Aren't I awful?" or to inflict self-blame or guilt. Rather, it is to know and take responsibility for how that part of you impacts and influences others as well as yourself. Then you can set an intention of managing and healing the angry, hurtful one within.

In Mack's case, he was the killer, the enemy and the destroyer. He was also the hunted, the ally and the rescuer. What he had disowned was his inherent softness, compassion, vulnerability and trust. To reach a full appreciation of all he was, Mack had to access and re-own the lost parts of himself that he had cut off in Vietnam. He desperately needed to claim the lost boy, and the hero, within himself.

Another reason for working through trauma in a safe environment is to help reclaim the lost parts of yourself you may have left behind. Once you become aware of them, you can more easily integrate them into your personality to enable you to become whole and fully functional.

As I contemplated what Mack really needed, I was motivated to create an exquisite exact moment of healing for him. Much of his experience in Vietnam had to do with his physical being—his endurance and exhaustion; the relentless pain in his feet and back; the sound of guns, bombs and pouring rain all played against the deadly silence of listening for the approaching enemy. The stench of jungle life and war, compounded by the constant threat to his life, placed every fiber and cell of his body under siege.

Certainly, it was not possible to totally simulate Vietnam. I decided that some physical activity here and now would be critical to trigger the body memory of his experience in the jungle. I chose his experience of carrying the radio, because he carried it for over a year, and it remains a prominent and constant reality of that time period. Even now, he has back pain and residual body trauma as a result of carrying the weight—not only of the physical radio, but also as the lifeline for his whole troop. As I was considering this, Mack provided the detail I needed.

"When the guy carrying the radio got shot in the head, I volunteered to carry it. At that point, I had been in Vietnam only about a month. I was sent to a secured military area, where I took a week-long crash course in how to operate the equipment. After training, I went back to my unit, which had been assigned to go up north and serve as a special landing force scouting Vietcong in the jungles.

"Carrying the radio was a tremendous physical challenge because of the excess weight. The radio equipment weighed about forty pounds. Together with my other gear, the whole pack weighed about ninety pounds. I was also emotionally affected. The radio was our lifeline. Without it, we'd be dead. It created a lot of fear in me.

"I have had physical problems related to my back that stemmed from that time. I've had two serious back surgeries, and have done a lot of personal work around this. An awareness I get out of my body is that a lot of times when I'm talking about emotionally-charged issues in my life, I immediately feel a pain in my back.

"I specifically remember my first time serving as the radioman. My unit was on one of its first patrols in the jungle. For safety, we were told to walk about fifteen or twenty yards apart. That was to keep injuries to a minimum, in case there were land mines. All of a sudden, one of the guys walking about fifty yards up from where I was, stepped on a mine. I remember hearing the explosion and hearing him scream. Everything went crazy at that point. Everyone was screaming for the radioman. When I got to the scene, I saw that both his legs, one of his arms and the hand on his other arm were blown off. There was blood everywhere.

"We later found his boot, with his foot still in it. This was the first guy I ever saw get wounded, and this was the first time I had had to perform my duties as radioman. I was panicked and really afraid of hearing him hollering and screaming and seeing how mangled he was. I had to call the medivac chopper and, in my fear and panic, I was forgetting how to do it. You have to get on a certain frequency, give grid coordinates of your location, and tell them if there's any hostile fire. My hands were shaking so bad I could hardly turn the dials. I remember thinking that I was not going to get out of there alive.

"From that day forward, I became hypersensitive and vigilant looking for booby traps. We walked in the jungle day in and day out, for miles and miles. Every step I took, I always feared my next one was going to be on a land mine. I was never without fear or anxiety about this."

By this time, Mack had the only dry eyes in the room. For me, this powerful story contained the image that signaled to me, "This is it. Go with it." I instructed Irene, his student facilitator, to have Mack select someone in the group who might be around the same weight as the radio pack. He chose a petite woman who weighed around 90 pounds. She willingly clung to his back piggyback style, wrapping her legs around him.

To carry the added weight he had to bend forward, hunch his back and position his legs wider apart than usual in order to balance the load. He did this automatically and efficiently. We witnessed the precision of an expert. The moment that he felt the weight on his back, his facial expression changed. We saw a furrowed brow, heavy with responsibility. His face reflected what his entire body was experiencing—the fear, the physical discomfort, the single-mindedness of his mission, the unfailing determination, along with incredible, unrelenting exhaustion.

I asked Mack to march around the room in that condition without stopping. He circled the room with the 90-pound woman gripping his shoulders and clinging to his back. I told the rest of the people in the room to simulate what he reported as his own inner voice. They yelled things like "Keep going soldier. You can't stop.

Stop and you die. Drop that radio and we're all dead." Mack marched around and around—I had the feeling he could have circled the room indefinitely. He remembered being cold, hot, wet, dry. Stench of death. Dirty. In that moment, this impeccably dressed man remembered going 6 months without a shower. It didn't matter. Nothing mattered. He would have carried on, carrying the radio. I don't know exactly how long Mack marched around that room, but I felt pain in his every step. At one point, I told Mack the war was over and that we would stop when he chose to go no further. He put down the woman and fell to the floor moaning.

"I'm tired. I'm so tired. I'm so fucking tired. Help me. My back hurts."

I encouraged people to kneel in a circle around Mack, and to gently begin touching and massaging his back. A reverential silence filled the room, broken only by Mack's continued laments.

"I hate myself. I lost so much time. I want to feel my heart again."

By having a safe space, filled with emotionally responsive loving people, Mack could afford to be vulnerable and have authentic emotional responses. He expressed his outrage, sobbed, shook in terror, and experienced his deepest despair at the enormous loss of precious friends. In this corrective manner and in the safety of the training group, he finally was able to access his grief, allow the tears to flow, and thereby begin his healing process. Everyone in the group consoled him. Each person seemed to have complete understanding and acceptance, and offered unconditional love.

When you have life experiences of loss, separation and death that you never mourn, you deny yourself the natural and healthy vehicle of grieving. Active grieving enables you to digest what seems indigestible, and to release what will hurt if you don't let it go. Sadly, many in our culture view tears of grieving as weakness, especially Marines. They preach a "stiff upper lip" as the most respectable and expected response to grief. However, people who deny themselves the right to cry, wail and rage in a safe environment, are then forced to swallow their toxic experience and carry it in their guts, thus souring and limiting many future experiences.

Psychotherapies limited to talking about experiences often fail to help clients access their grief that, in most cases, has been buried under layers and years of rationalization and denial. By creating a safe, responsive space where clients can physically and emotionally revisit their trauma and "change the outcome," I can empower them to discover for themselves the vital solution to what has been crippling their lives. I believe that as you are hurt by experience, so do you heal by experience.

Some of the time he was silent. Later he would reveal to us that in those moments, scenes of his life were passing before his eyes— moments that needed healing. I asked Mack what he needed and wanted in this moment—right here and now to help him feel safe.

He paused, closing his eyes and shaking his head as if he couldn't believe what he had just discovered and was about to reveal.

"I want my mom. I want to be cradled. I want to feel safe in my mother's arms. I want to feel her love and protection. I want to love and accept myself."

I was surprised to hear Mack's need for his mother emerge at this point to the foreground. Although I had heard of dying soldiers crying out for their mothers or fathers, here was a live veteran with the same personal needs. It struck me that Mack's mother had died when he was a young teen and that he had loved her deeply. I am still fascinated and humbled by the critical importance of the therapist staying out of the way and following the client so that he can discover his real need as the truth emerges out of the work.

It is not coincidental that all the memories of death Mack was having would stimulate the experience of the most important death in his life, that of his mother. How did he get to his mother? The longings and sobbing, about the horror of mutilated men led him to the excruciatingly painful death of his mother.

In Mack's case, there was still more grieving to do about her death, a death not fully mourned. It was a raw wound that he still carried. He needed a deep spiritual/emotional reconnection to his mother.

I asked all the women in the group to form two lines and interlock arms, forming a human cradle in which Mack could be held and rocked. Specially selected music played a crucial role at this emotional juncture. I selected Carol King's "Child of Mine," and encouraged the women to hold and rock Mack. He continued the chant. "Help me Mommy, I miss you." Everyone was crying, especially Mack, who finally felt the soothing power of his own tears.

After we had all cried what felt like a river of tears, we gently put Mack down and asked him to return to the center of the circle. One by one, each person thanked him from the bottom of his or her heart and acknowledged his sacrifice and honored him as the war hero that he was and is. Through a great stream of tears, Mack told us, "I have waited 25 years for this."

It was important for all the women to stand in and form a mothering cradle. Mack learned that, when held in loving arms, the unbearable images of dying men could be endured. He could safely get it expressed, out and released from the imprisonment of his body, where he was holding the trauma.

Then Tim, who had dodged the draft, stepped into the circle, hugged Mack and said, "Welcome home, Mack, and thank you." Mack and Tim cried in one another's arms. I'll never forget that sight. Men who had taken actively opposing positions on the war, each of whom had suffered enormous consequences for his choices, now were converging as two men offering mutual respect and understanding. Each was getting another piece of what he needed. It was a moment within a moment of healing.

This deep spontaneous and supportive response from the group was critical to Mack's healing. At that moment, we were all civilians thanking him, honoring and respecting him, expressing our enormous empathy and gratitude to him for the gift of service he had given every one of us.

The experience impacted everyone in the room so deeply that there was a noticeable hesitation to bring closure to the experience. I allowed people to linger, while, one by one, they made their comments to Mack.

A while later, in talking about his first "exact moment" of healing, Mack told me:

"It was the turning point for me. This was the first time in my life I felt important—that people were listening to me. I continued to create healing moments throughout my training, and each time I felt validated and honored as a person, and as a therapist. Now I feel emotionally cleansed and healed. I feel love, and am finally in charge of my life.

"When I think back on Vietnam, and the years I spent addicted to alcohol and drugs, a part of me still marvels at how I got out of it alive. But now, there's this bigger part of me that understands the spiritual side. My guardian angels were there with me in those dark holes, and they probably were saying, 'You aren't goin' anywhere. You have work to do for others.'"

Mack emerged as one of the most outstanding students in his class. His perceptions and clinical skills proved to be so keen that I often was amazed by his ability to guide clients to the heart of their issues. Mack had studied and worked very hard in the program. In addition, there was something special about him, a rare vision and compassion that went far beyond academic understanding. It is my belief that Mack's destiny had pushed him to the "edge," and he had come back with amazing grace.

Grief and the Boomerang

Whenever you suffer a major loss, you will need to go through a grieving process that involves waves of sorrow, anger and disbelief. Mack's whole being longed to release the grief and to be heard and comforted by empathetic friends and loved ones. If you are not safe to do that, as in Mack's case in Vietnam, then you must stuff it, pretend it doesn't hurt, tough it out and go on. Unfortunately, this does not dissolve the grief; it stays lodged in you like a rock. Think about your history. Have you experienced any major loss? If so, how have you responded? Do you believe you've fully grieved the loss? Have you received what you need to resolve it? If not, what do you still need to express to someone?

Remember, retroflection is doing to you what you would like to do or say to another. When you resist grieving, you retroflect all that energy, hold it in your body, cut off parts of yourself and essentially put yourself in harm's way. When Mack came home from Vietnam, he had all his aggression activated, with no place to put it. And he had tremendous survival guilt and enormous grief locked within; in short, a hurricane of emotional energy looking for a place to land. It took tremendous force to contain all that energy within his body. It needed releasing, and instead got turned back against himself. The full force boomeranged and hit him, resulting in depression and addiction. He became his own target. In short, he was now the enemy. Mack needed a safe place to express all his pain, sorrow and anger about the war and the loss of his comrades and his mother.

Think about the last time you were really angry. Remember the body sensations; the clenching of your teeth, the tightening in your chest, the rush of blood flow. That energy needs to go someplace—out or in; outside or inside your body. If you're angry with someone, and don't have the skills or opportunity to express that anger, you may reverse the flow of this powerful emotion. Instead of directing it outward, you may turn on yourself via criticizing, shaming, constricting, tightening or confining. "I hate myself for being in this situation" or "I hate my body." You put your hand through a wall or a plate glass window in anger. You hurt yourself. Your body receives the blow. If you have unexpressed anger or unmourned loss, be careful that, like Mack, you have not buried it under some addictive behavior, or allowed yourself to slip into depression.

In order to be heard, respected and provided for, your anger and sorrow needs to be skillfully delivered. Remember, anger needs to go out, never in. Grief needs to flow like a river. Find a way to healthfully express your anger, and release your sorrow. Get help from a therapist. Hit a punching bag, or scream into a pillow. Cry into the arms of a loving friend. Do no harm to yourself or to anyone else while still respecting your heart's anguish.

Start by doing what's necessary; then do what's possible; and suddenly you are doing the impossible.

—St. Francis of Assisi

Chapter Six

ROBIN—FACING THE PAIN

"The day that I was supposed to leave for Mariah's workshop, Stefan, my youngest son, had a fever. He had an inoperable brain tumor, and was now on chemotherapy with a catheter in his chest. We thought he had an infection, so my husband and I brought him to the emergency room.

"Even though I was under duress, I knew if I wanted to attend the weekend workshop, I had to leave. It was not a conflict. I just knew I had to go, not really knowing why I had to go. I just left them there in the emergency room, and drove nearly five hours to get myself there.

"Stefan required a lot of things—medically, educationally, psychologically. And, we had two other kids as well. I kept myself busy doing it all—I wasn't really alive, but I didn't realize that. I wasn't aware of anything other than I had to get help. When I arrived at the workshop, I didn't know there were going to be thirty people. Then there were all these boxes of tissues—which I thought was odd. "

Robin was referred to me by my close friend and colleague, Dr. Mark Putnam. Robin and her husband, Charlie, were long-time friends of his who, for the previous 2 years, had been dealing with the tragedy of their young son, Stefan, who was diagnosed with a rare and inoperable brain tumor just before his fourth birthday. It threatened his vision and his life.

Before I met Robin and Charlie, Mark had told me about these two remarkable people with keen minds and sensitive hearts and a capacity for prolonged and deep commitment. True to their respective characters, they each responded to their son's diagnosis with love and dignity. They thoroughly researched the disease and obtained the best medical options. At the same time, they opened themselves to spiritual and emotional sustenance and wisdom.

I have found it to be true that those who live their lives in a full and healthy way cope with crisis in a similar manner. They rise to the occasion and become better people for it. Certainly, Robin and Charlie are two such people. Robin and Charlie each consecutively attended one of my weekend workshops.

Slightly built, with blondish hair, in her late thirties and casually dressed, Robin easily transmitted her kindness through her warm face and eyes. When I met her, I had the feeling I had known her a long time; there was an immediate, distinctive connection. I would describe her as an earth-mother type—one who makes everyone in the room feel important and cared for. She was what I call an *emotional leader*—every group needs at least one of them. They are the emotional glue that helps create and maintain cohesion and a supportive and trustworthy environment.

With her soft voice, Robin was articulate and moving when she spoke. Her story continues:

"I did hot seat work on the last day—Sunday, and I fretted all Saturday night about what I was going to work on. I wanted to do it right, but I wasn't exactly sure what that meant. I decided to work on why I don't take care of myself. Why don't I do the things that are good for me and that I enjoy? I know what I need, but I don't do any of it, and I wanted to know why.

"As I was explaining that to the people in the workshop, I said, 'Oh, by the way, something else is going on in my life. I have a son who is 4 years old, has a brain tumor and is going through chemotherapy.' I said it as if it were a postscript; as if that could ever be a postscript—ever. Mariah said immediately, 'Let's work on that.' I answered, 'No, I don't want to work on that; I can get to that pain any time. I'd rather work on something I can't get to.'

"Mariah encouraged me to trust her. 'You'll see,' she said, 'they're related.'"

It's not unusual for people who come to the workshop with a

125

critical issue to actually block out why they are there. I've seen people who finally have invited a family member or spouse—sometimes after years of preparation—get up to the open seat and present a totally unrelated issue. Their fear causes them to freeze up and figuratively go deaf, dumb and blind.

"I was so scared—shaking in my shoes. I didn't know what was going to happen. I'm basically a shy person, and I was in front of a lot of people. I didn't know exactly what I was supposed to do. I started talking and I thought I was just babbling. I just didn't know.

"When the topic turned to Stefan, I started talking about motherhood, and the related changes motherhood made in me—the shifts in philosophy. I was a hippie, a pacifist. I thought the kind and right thing to do in a situation, if I had to kill or be killed, would be to be killed. Killing is wrong. When I had my first child, that was the moment I knew I had the capacity to kill without hesitation in order to protect my child.

"The other knowledge was that I would suffer the worst pain in the world if something happened to this child, any child of mine, any child of any mother—this has got to be the worst pain. And that is what I'm living with because my son's tumor is lethal to him. I can't believe that I have to face my worst fear in life."

I asked Robin to pick someone to stand in for Stefan. She picked her dear friend Mark Putnam, because she said he knew Stefan and would know what to say. I wanted her to have an experience of complete freedom to say anything and everything that she might have locked away inside her as her way of sparing Stefan and Charlie the depth of her fear and sorrow. I knew all this needed to come out, that she needed to let that pain and fear pour out of her so that it would not hold her in its vise grip.

"I don't know if it was a conscious decision to let myself feel this. I was in the flow of the moment, allowing Mariah

whatever she wanted to do—her goal definitely was to get me to the heart of my pain and make me feel it. It's not, 'There, there Robin, let's make it better. Don't cry.' Mariah's approach encourages you to just cry and cry— and cry harder. She wants you to cry until you get every last bit out. That's the healing part. That's what's different."

I asked Robin to tell Stefan what was in her heart and encouraged her to hold him. She spontaneously cradled her son, as she must have done when he was a baby. Seeing her, holding her ailing child in her arms, appeared to me as a contemporary living Pieta. In myself, I could feel the agony of a mother—all mothers— who must stand by helplessly watching as their children suffer. That's my worst nightmare. I can think of no greater pain than that of losing a child, or having that child's life or well-being threatened. This was one of those moments when I didn't know if I could contain my own feelings. Silently, I prayed for assistance to provide the most perfect experience possible. I knew all of it, even this moment, was in the truest sense out of my hands.

"I began to speak to Stefan and really cry. 'I love you more than I can ever say in words. My pain is in trying to let you go. I don't want to let you go. I'm really feeling so afraid of losing you. And loving you. You are such a beautiful child and so brave. How could this be happening to you? It isn't fair.'"

At one point, as Robin was sobbing, she let out a wail of sorrow so deep and loud that it took me by surprise. I shuddered; even the most reserved person in the room was moved to tears. People were holding one another and pouring forth compassion and support. It permeated the air with everyone breathing it in. People were carrying her pain. It became our pain.

She had to touch down into the core of her pain, the burning cauldron if you will, and release it, so it did not consume her. It needed to be released from her and put into the universe with us as its carriers.

"I was letting go of everything and letting myself feel whatever was there. Most of the time I had my eyes closed,

but at one point, I opened my eyes and saw all these people around me, and they were all crying with me. It was like looking in the mirror. I was feeling compassion for them, as they were for me. I guess it was compassion for myself. Letting myself feel this pain had been way too big for me to look at or touch alone.

"Toward the end, Mariah asked me, 'What do you need?' And I said, 'I need to feel.' And that was the first time I realized that. In that moment, it came effortlessly to me. If you asked me if there was a goal for the workshop, I'd say there wasn't one, but my organism was saying, 'You need to feel and this is how you're going to do it.'"

Robin had been an abundant source, a well from which her family could draw whatever they needed. I now needed to feed that source, to nourish and replenish her, as well as provide her an experience that would teach her now how to comfort herself, and refuel in the future. I had everyone surround her while the 12 people closest to her lifted her forming a human cradle. They rocked her to "Bridge Over Troubled Water."

"I heard Mariah ask me, 'What color do you see as healing?' I said, 'Blue,' and within what seemed like 5 seconds, she pulled out this beautiful blue satin sheet and covered me with it. To my amazement, as I let this in, my heart opened even further."

I wanted Robin to have a dynamic memory of this moment, so that she could draw on it anytime she needed comfort or strength. With that in mind, I designed the work to touch her on all physical levels—kinesthetic, auditory and visual, as well as on psycho-spiritual levels.

"I was empowered to release and relax and trust that I wasn't going to die, and that everything was just as it should be. It wasn't a matter of keeping it all together, doing everything I was supposed to do. It was a matter of letting go.

"In that moment, I felt that, even if the worst thing happened, and Stefan were overcome by this tumor, I could survive. I had made a shift. I trusted in that moment that I had enough faith in God, in my beliefs about life and death and in the people around me to love me through it. I realized that the people in my life are amazing in how they make me feel—that it will all work out, that I can be carried through this and that there isn't anything too big for the human spirit and the love of the people close to me. I don't think anyone can do this alone.

"I was in heaven; I just let in all that love and healing. By the end of the workshop, I was definitely in an altered state of mind. It was a 4 1/2 hour trip home and it seemed like an hour.

"Before developing a background in psychology, I believed that flight was right, that you should avoid intense emotional pain, try to control it or transcend it through meditation, for the sake of self-preservation. I've gradually grown to see the flaws in this belief. My experience at the workshop confirmed that if you don't allow yourself to feel the pain, you cannot feel the joy either. I think that if you allow yourself to feel pain, and feel it fully, you can be transformed.

"When that emotional pain is happening to me, it's a physical feeling of intense pain in my heart and chest. The first time I had that feeling was when I was in love with Charlie, and we broke up. The second time was in that workshop, when I was crying about Stefan. In the past 4 or 5 years, when that feeling has come up, I'm no longer afraid of it. By feeling it totally, I know I'm doing something good for myself. I try to do what Mariah showed me: to get it all out, get it all out as much as I can. Whether I'm in my bedroom or in the woods, I'll do whatever I have to or go wherever I have to go to get to the pain and release it.

"When I'm done, I surround myself with angels and love and green; these days my healing color is green. I breathe all that in just the way Mariah had everyone do for me at the weekend. That's something I learned there: not to be afraid of the physical sensation of emotional pain—to dive right into it, try to get it out, and then love myself afterwards.

"I also learned to pay more attention to my body, to all its little aches and pains, and try to associate a message. My body's talking to me; it's trying to tell me something. I try to listen more because I know that if I take care of my body, my body will take care of me. I mean that in a big way, on a spiritual level."

It's not widely understood that each of us is "dyadic" in our nature, that is, we both experience and respond to our experiences and thoughts. We actually are in a relationship with ourselves. When you think, for instance, you are essentially talking to yourself. Then you respond via your body. It's a twofold process. When you have critical thoughts about yourself, you almost always respond with bodily tension and hurt feelings, thus compounding the negative impact. If you cry and you have the thought that crying is wrong or weak, or you respond with indifference instead of empathy and love for yourself, then you, in fact, increase the original sorrow.

It's important to mention here that when you avoid the more painful emotions—grief, sorrow, anger, frustration, fear and dread—you also diminish your ability to feel excitement, joy, sexuality, peace and safety. You train your organism to live life on the flat plane. On the other hand, expressing intense emotion is not enough. There are many people who cry and wail and never heal, because they are crying into a vacuum, they cry alone rather than "with themselves." There is no inner voice to respond and comfort them. They create the experience of no one caring. No one is home.

I cannot emphasize enough the importance of developing a positive relationship with yourself. I spend a lot of time with all of my clients, training them how to be in a loving, responsive, active relationship with themselves and how to develop a positive internal dialogue. I wait until I'm sure they have integrated enough internal support before I embark on any deep work with them. Without this core strength, they might cry or rage on the surface and never resolve issues or heal—rendering the work ineffective.

This concept is essential. Full intensity of emotion is not the primary goal. However, it is feeling and responding to the emotion received by ourselves and others that makes the critical difference. Mourning and grieving in a vacuum or in an uncaring environment can add more pain to the injury. It is important for anyone who is facing deep pain to learn how to respond immediately to him or herself with understanding, compassion and an embrace. I frequently tell my clients, "When you cry, cry into your own embrace." This may take the form of a physical embrace, where you put your arms around yourself in the same spirit as you would comfort a loved one. It's also ideal if there is a person or people who provide a receptive, emotionally generous environment. This is what I create in the workshop setting, providing a laboratory for clients to experiment and learn new behaviors.

It was clear to me that Robin had enough self-support to enter the excruciating grief held tightly below her surface. It was also clear that the rest of the people in the workshop, and I, were feeling a spontaneous and genuine collective sorrow and a desire to embrace her. Thus, all the essential conditions for safety and potential transformation were met.

During her first exact moment of healing, she squarely faced all the pain and anxiety surrounding her son's illness. It proved to be a heartfelt transformation for her and everyone who worked along with her in the workshop.

Your Relationship with You

Your relationship with yourself lies at the heart of all healing and provides the foundation upon which a good partnership rests. It is unfair and impossible to ask a partner to love you better or more than you love yourself. You will sabotage that love. You will not allow it in at a very deep level.

By loving yourself, I don't mean narcissism or selfishness or self-inflated views of yourself. I mean that you are in contact with yourself. You are in your body, in your mind with your heart and soul. You are in total contact with and appreciate the four aspects of yourself: the physical, the emotional, the spiritual and the intellectual.

It's also important for you to have unconditional love for yourself and a steady flow of compassion not only for all your hurts and pains but also for any illnesses, weaknesses, flaws and insecurities. And it's critical that you have forgiveness for yourself. That doesn't mean in any way lowering your standards of morality or ethics. It means you are human. When you fall down, you need to be the first one there to pick yourself up. It means having an active internal dialogue, talking to yourself in very loving ways. You are, in fact, talking to yourself morning, noon and night via thinking. If you're having a monologue as if you were talking to no one, you'll end up feeling lonely. You'll have loneliness within rather than being in relationship with yourself.

We are relational beings. We exist and behave in relationship to something or someone. This phenomenon of relating, so beautifully described by the philosopher Martin Buber, requires both an I and a Thou. So I, Mariah, see and value you, Mariah. I don't mean that there is more than one of me. What I mean is that I am both the seer and the object of my seeing. I'm only one. I both touch myself lovingly and am touched by myself. So, the more you can develop this close, active relationship with yourself, the healthier and happier you will become.

That means talking to yourself purposefully. Turn a lot of your thinking into personal conversation with yourself. There is someone home. Live as if you're at home with yourself. Stand by yourself. Don't be alone. Instead, be with yourself and develop the internal relationship that you want externally, because usually what you have is a match. What's inside is outside. You attract what you are. And, unfortunately, you cannot, over time, allow in any more love than you are already giving to yourself.

So, develop an inner dialogue that is very rich. Every night, I have this moment with myself. In my bathroom, I surrounded the tub with floor to ceiling mirrors, so that I and Thou can chat. I give myself appreciation for what I have done that day. How I have lived another day well. Or, maybe I have to forgive myself when I am less than kind or patient or when I'm tough or critical or all those human things that we all can be.

For a moment, look at your hands. Look at each finger, the front, and the back. Consider for a moment that you ARE your hands, instead of your HAVING hands. They are not separate from you. You ARE your hands. Think back, over time, of all the things your hands have done for you. Thank your hands. What are the most valuable things your hands do for you? Thank them. Remember that you were born into this life with these same hands.

Now imagine you're looking in a mirror at your own face. Look into your own eyes. See the emotion in your eyes. Say your own name out loud. Keep saying it. For example, "Mariah, I am with you now and always. I will never abandon you. And if it takes our whole lifetime, I will learn to love you well. You have my deep commitment."

Now in this moment, ask yourself, using your own name, what do you feel now? And wait for an answer.

When you have your answer, ask what do you need about that from me right now. And now, provide what you need. Give it to yourself.

And now, receive what you have given. Inhale. Receive. And thank yourself.

I will review these four steps with you. Look in a mirror and use your own first name.

1. Ask yourself, "(Your Name), what do you feel now?" (Wait for an answer)
2. Ask yourself, "(Your Name), what do you want or need from me about that feeling now?" (Wait for an answer)
3. Creatively provide
4. Receive and appreciate what you have provided

Eventually, you will want to develop the ability to imagine your own face as clearly as if you were looking in a mirror. Can you imagine a white and yellow daisy? Now, imagine your own face. Is it more difficult? Usually it's nearly impossible before you've done a lot of this work. You don't know your own face instantly. You want to be able to visualize yourself as clearly as if you were in a mirror, and that will take some time.

Is speaking to yourself with kindness a new experience? If so, that's the intimacy missing. And that's exciting, because as you do this, your life is going to absolutely change.

And here's the wonderful thing. Like Robin, you'll come to your other relationships already loved. You'll arrive full, and others will find you easy to love. You're not coming "on empty." That's really, really important. Do not expect a partner to give you any more than you're giving yourself. Arrive already loved.

Charlie—Sharing the Pain

I am of the opinion that my life belongs to the whole community and
as long as I live, it is my privilege to do for it whatever I can.
I want to be thoroughly used up when I die
—for the harder I work the more I love.

—George Bernard Shaw

Chapter Seven

CHARLIE—SHARING THE PAIN

*"As I was driving to the workshop, I was extremely anxious.
I didn't know exactly what to expect, nor did I really
understand what I was going through. Halfway there, I
realized that I was scared to death. As I continued the
journey, I settled into my body and resigned myself to trust,
and to be open to whatever was going to happen. Whatever
I discovered, I felt that I would be able to accept and live
through it. I needed that 4 1/2 hour drive to get to that
point.*

*"I didn't really have a goal. I had been going through quite
an ordeal with both my son and my wife's health. My
emotional state at that point was dominated by trying to
keep up with everything."*

Robin's exact moment of healing was a crucial turning point in
her life, and it would prove to be training ground for yet another
huge challenge. About a year later, her husband Charlie came to one
of my weekend workshops, and revealed that Robin had been
diagnosed with advanced breast cancer. It's not unusual when a
person suffers a major loss or tragedy for her to develop a major
illness. I don't know whether or not this is true in Robin's case.
Regardless, I now had a family under siege on two fronts. Although
Robin's cancer went into remission, the weight of bearing up under
such dire circumstances, and the prospect of losing both his wife and
son were at the core of Charlie's exact moment of healing.

Charlie, about 6 feet tall, with brown hair and pine brown eyes,
had a smile that emanated genuineness. He stayed in the background
and was not one to command attention. In fact, when he spoke, it
was clear he was strong, reliable, very intelligent and one who
ponders things deeply.

"When I arrived, walking into the room was truly uplifting. There were group exercises with music, looking at each person in the room, sharing and learning a little about one another. That sort of allayed my fears, because I felt this was the beginning of the process, and we were starting to know everyone and feel connected.

"One of the first exercises was about our early family life. I remembered going through the list of my experiences, talking about my childhood—the fact that my brothers and sisters were a lot older than I was. They were already living away from home during most of my formative years. I felt so connected when they came home for Christmas because normally I was an 'only child.' That started my being aware of how important it is for me to feel connected to people, to humanity—to everyone. That set the tone for the issue that I addressed later.

"Mariah reminds everyone that, even if you come to the workshop with a goal, whatever's happening at the time is what's happening, and that's what you have to feel."

By early Saturday afternoon, three people in the group had done their individual work. Charlie openly wept with compassion for them and for what I imagined to be his own intense agony. I rarely tell people when to do their individual work. In Charlie's case, however, he was obviously primed. I wanted him to experience relief as soon as possible and give his body the break it needed. I wanted him to "ex-press" or press out the pain, stress and terror that he was containing. That clearing could enable him to use the rest of the weekend for healing and connecting with and receiving from caring people. I knew he would need a lot of "filling up" for when he returned home to bear his unbearable sorrow. So I gave him a nod of invitation to begin his work now.

"I remember looking at Mariah as she motioned for me to come up. I certainly needed that. She told me later that it was highly unusual for her to do that. She usually wants people to step forward on their own. I was grateful for her

encouragement; it felt like the right thing to do. I sat in the open seat, surrounded by all those glowing faces. Mariah asked in her usual fashion, what's important and some other very pointed questions. From the moment I sat down, there was no anxiety left. I was a mass of feeling and energy, not self-conscious at all. That was a result of almost a day of being with the group and the power of the moment.

"She asked me what had been going on in my life. I poured forth my story which started the ball rolling. First, my son had been diagnosed with a tumor in his optic nerve just before his fourth birthday. That was quite an ordeal in itself. The nightmare continued when he went for chemotherapy. Six months later, my wife was diagnosed with breast cancer.

"I had been going through the motions, and doing whatever I felt I needed to do in order to maintain our family during this horrendous time. I spoke to doctors and nurses on an intellectual level, trying to understand everything but not feeling anything. I was concerned about what was going on with my wife and son and trying to make sure that whatever needed to be done was taken care of. I didn't consciously think about my personal emotional state. It had to be put aside. I wouldn't have realized that if anyone asked me how I was dealing with the traumas of my life.

"Now, as I related the details of Stefan's and Robin's illnesses, I finally was crying, and feeling a mass of emotion through it all. Mariah asked me what I needed. I said I felt as though I needed to curl up into a ball and be protected. She made that happen. I was curled up in the middle of the floor sobbing, letting go of sounds, words and thoughts that had been locked inside me without my knowing they were there. The whole group surrounded me and held me."

Charlie was in the middle of the circle curled around himself yelling, actually wailing, the words "No, No, No, not my Stefan!

Not my Robin! God, No. It can't be real!" And then, "Help me, help me, somebody, God help me!" I thought I might break along with him, as I imagined what he must be feeling, what he must be going through day after day, night after night, unable to save the lives of the people he treasured and was supposed to protect with his love.

To really have empathy, I must walk in my client's shoes in my imagination. Yet, I could hardly tolerate a second of imagining the horror in my own family if my husband and one of my sons had life-threatening illnesses. Immediately, I thought of my husband Ron who was in a situation similar to Charlie's. He, too, had been carrying a heavy burden with my ALS over these past many years. He has bravely and generously partnered with me in this life with ALS—the myriad times I've choked, fallen, broken fingers and teeth, arms and vertebrae, been stitched, stayed in emergency rooms, hospitals and rehabs, not to mention living in the ever-present shadow of death. It was getting harder for me to walk anywhere on my own, to dress myself, to stand or to feed myself. I physically needed more and more, and Ron was always there, protecting, loving and capable. Both these men were carrying the weight of their worlds, putting one foot in front of the other, like surefooted Sherpas, with love in their backpacks, making the climb before them.

I wondered about the toll on my sons, Luke and Cole, who carry on like brave soldiers, and have become gentlemen before their time. I wept for them, for Charlie, Robin, Stefan and Stefan's brothers—for all of us, for all families ravaged by disease and illness.

At moments like this, I also consider my illness an asset. If I can survive ALS, others can survive as well. I know the journey, its pitfalls and arduous climbs, its moments of terror and deep vulnerability. These experiences, when delivered to the heart of a compassionate other, can provide a moment like no other, of sweet connection and serenity.

I also know that illness cannot be well-carried alone. I used to consider myself fiercely independent. ALS brought me to my knees, teaching me how to depend on others and to ask for help. It has been humbling, as well as enriching, to give in to the ways of interdependence. Charlie was a bit lost in his isolation. I know that place of aloneness and isolation and how critical it is to break out of confinement into connectedness with people and something larger than ourselves.

I kept encouraging Charlie to say more, tell me more, and let out what was inside—to say it all. I could feel and see the enormous outpouring of compassion in the people whom I asked to move in and surround Charlie. Their hearts were open. While they held Charlie in their eyes and arms, they, too, grieved their own sorrows. He was in our protection. I played Albinoni's "Adagio in G minor."

"The music was perfect. I felt so able to release—such ecstasy because I could be released from my burden, and all those people were willing to help me with this. I felt a tremendous amount of trust, energy and love being put forth supporting me, an invisible but palpable energy. I could almost float on it."

In Robin's work, she needed to deepen her connection with herself. Charlie needed to work on his relatedness, and to reach out to the community of others. In this life, we're so often helpless with no forum to reach out to those we love and who are in crisis. In my workshops, I create a space where everyone contributes and helps to carry the pain of the person doing the work. In so doing, they are involved, truly helping, and knowing they are making a difference in someone's life. This labor of community touches people deeply—it is heart work, it is felt deep within.

We stayed with Charlie in that cocoon pile in the middle of the floor for quite a while, as his grief and anguish poured out. While the song "Amazing Grace" soothed us, I kept my hands lovingly on Charlie's head and heart as the waves of his emotions rose and fell. I prayed for him and his family and asked people in the room to say a prayer in their own way for Charlie and his loved ones to be protected. We were protecting him now, as we became a human cocoon around him. When his grieving subsided naturally, I asked Charlie to open his eyes and look around. He saw the eyes wet with tears for him, and all the arms embracing him. I told him to concentrate and precisely etch this moment into his memory forever so that he could draw on our love any time he needed us. I told him to purposefully inhale fully, breathing in all the support around him; to breathe it into every cell, every organ and every limb of his body until his entire being could become a sponge with every pore an active receptor. I wanted to maximize his receptivity in the moment, knowing that I was simultaneously training him how to do the same for himself later.

"Prior to the workshop, I felt alone. Because of my experience growing up as the isolated youngest child, I did everything on my own. I didn't realize how much I needed to connect to other people—to not feel so alone. I don't think I had much of an inkling of that before the workshop. My bond with Mariah reinforced the importance of connection for me. The realization of this is absolutely an ongoing process; sometimes I slip back into isolated functioning and forget to connect in the normal ebb and flow of life. Staying connected is something I must purposefully work on—to feel that there's something or someone else there for me. When I feel that connection to the world at large, I realize we're all here supporting each other. In those moments, I feel most alive."

The workshop helped Charlie realize that connecting with people can be life-sustaining for him, and make him feel complete. The experience also awakened his emotional responses about what was happening to him and his family and gave him a safe haven in which to reveal them.

Out of Isolation into Connectedness

Charlie, like Atlas, felt he had to carry the weight of the world on his shoulders. When the lives of his beloved wife and son were threatened, the weight became unbearable. Think about a time when you were heartbroken and burdened with a powerful issue and then isolated yourself. How did that feel? Even if you have developed a loving relationship with yourself, you will still have, as a social being, a profound longing to be known and cared for. In Charlie's case, there was a desperate silent scream locked inside—please help me!

If you tend to isolate in times of personal pain, know that this aloneness can harden you, and create a vacuum within. This standing like a statue, arms crossed over your heart, holding your breath, can leave you vulnerable to depression, failed relationships, illness and lost possibilities. Outside the circle of love and light, you lose moments of sweet comfort and connectedness, look and feel sallow, sound flat or disgruntled.

Crisis isolationists arrive at my office disillusioned about other people and their own lives. They've forgotten their essential need for human interconnectedness and seem lost without a friend in the world. When I suggest a workshop, they are the first ones to say, "Oh no, I don't do groups." Of course, that's precisely why I recommend it. They may need to peel their hands and arms, one finger at a time, away from shielding their heart and find their way home to that place where we all unite.

Realize that you don't have to carry your burdens alone, even the smaller ones. There are people, a universe, and a God of your understanding, who will help. Ron used to say, "No, that's all right. I can do it," when someone, maybe even a stranger, offered help with my disability. When walking up steps or going through doors or getting in and out of a car, he took it as a personal challenge and a sign of his character and physical strength to do it himself. I encouraged him, over time, to say "yes" to offers of help and to be open to discovering what happens.

After years of independence, he realized he was missing moments, memories and exchanges with people. He began saying "yes," and enjoying the moment. Like the time we went to the movies and came out of the theater to realize it had snowed heavily. With me in a wheelchair, he had to negotiate opening snow-clogged doors, icy pathways and a blowing wind to get me to, and in, the van. When several strangers asked if they could help, he quickly accepted. He now remembers fondly the sweet moments of contact with them. As a result, we have hundreds of experiences with people we never would have met.

By sharing his need and pain, Charlie helped lift the barriers of separateness, and grounded us so that all our roots reached down to the same sacred soil. He moved us out of his and our isolation into relatedness, into a one-ness. He took that very delicate risk of sharing his deepest vulnerabilities and asking for a human intimate response. By receiving our empathy and support, he also gave to us and created a circle of nourishment. Charlie was our teacher that day, reminding us all that it is only by surrendering completely and accepting and expressing our vulnerabilities that we welcome and promote a heartfelt response from people in our world.

Tales of a Wounded Healer

No I would not give you false hope
On this strange and mournful day.
But the mother and child reunion
Is only a motion away.

—Paul Simon

Chapter Eight

JACK—REVISITING THE ASSUMPTIONS

"I'm reluctant to put myself out in front of people. And part of that, I know, is because of my own insecurities from what I perceive to be all the rejection and abandonment issues from my childhood. I was scared; I was very scared.

"When I first sat down next to Mariah in the hot seat, in front of the whole group, I began talking. Mariah—I know a lot of people say this about her—is so disarming and so 'right there' with you that, even though we were sitting facing this large group, quickly those people became 'out of focus.' They were there, supportive, and all paying close attention. However, I was only aware of Mariah and I sitting in the room."

I knew little about Jack when he sat down in the open seat. He was a nice-looking man in his mid-forties, with a quiet manner and kind, open face. During the workshop, he was attentive and responsive to people, yet he didn't stand out to make himself known. Rather, he connected to people one-on-one in a very supportive way and more or less stayed in the background.

It seemed to me that on the first day, Jack was ready to do individual work, yet he kept losing out to the more assertive people who managed to reach the seat before him. Finally, on the second day, he gathered his courage and sat down.

When he spoke, he knew precisely what he wanted to say. He told us that his early life had profoundly affected his adult functioning, and he wanted to address the unfinished business associated with his relationships with his mother, father and grandmother. I asked him to tell us about his childhood and to focus on what he felt was the most unresolved conflict from that period of time.

"I was only about 3 or 4 months old when my mother left my father and me, and my father took me to live with his mother—my grandmother. During those early years, I saw my mother infrequently, even though her house was only 500 yards from my elementary school. When I was 6 years old, I remember the day my mother and her father came to my grandmother's house in an effort to reclaim me. My grandmother and I were standing across the room from where my mother and her father stood, just inside the front door. They asked me if I wanted to come with them. My grandmother literally had me clutched to her bosom on the opposite side of the room. I remember feeling frozen in fear and confusion. The upshot was, I stayed there with my grandmother, and my mother and grandfather left. I never saw my mother again."

When Jack said the words, "I never saw my mother again," he was choked up. A profound silence fell over the room as each of us experienced the emptiness and loss that must have dominated this boy's life. The trauma of that past moment, and the resulting years of living with a chronic sense of abandonment, all surfaced at once. His trembling voice, his body curving over itself for protection, and his head hanging in his hands, all illustrated to me how much hurt he had carried for so long.

I was deeply saddened for him. Flooded with memories and feelings about the loss of my own father, I naturally identified strongly with his loss of a parent through abandonment and subsequent divorce. As a host of memories flashed by in an instant, my whole body resonated with Jack. When I was 2 1/2 years old, I awoke one morning and my mother told me my father, a man whom I adored, was gone and would never return. I wondered what I must have felt then. The loss was devastating to me, and I'm told by relatives that after my father left, I cried inconsolably for days on end. The consequences of this kind of loss can be, and were, long-lasting.

Growing up, I exhibited all the classic symptoms of an abandoned child; underlying depression, damaged self-worth and shattered trust. Early photographs of me show a cute little redheaded girl with a sorrowful face. My Aunt Ellie says I was the saddest little girl she had ever seen.

My depression showed itself early in my underachievement in school. I was academically anxious and had no confidence in myself. Here I was, having one of the highest IQs in the school, dead last in sixth grade. I created these enormous expectations of myself that accepted only excellence. If I couldn't be brilliant, then I was stupid. I went with stupid. It was a terrible dichotomy to live with.

Later, in my teens and twenties, I questioned whether life was worth living, whether I was at all lovable and able to create healthy relationships, and whether suicide was an alternative. My depression by this time was full-blown.

Because I also mistrusted all men, I ran through a series of relationships with them (after all, because I felt unlovable, I thought I'd leave them before they left me!). Finally, in a culmination of who I was at that time, I attached to someone who was profoundly depressed and constantly on the edge of suicide. I was in as deep as you can get. He finally killed himself and I didn't

These feelings added a whole new dimension to my relationship to Jack. On the one hand, I felt this deep soul connection to him. On the other hand, I was busy trying not to impose any of my own issues onto his work, keeping myself from getting in the way of a healthy therapeutic process. I had to remain the open-minded investigator, discovering along with him what his present feelings were with all their subtleties and intensity.

I was also aware that my deep personal knowing about this kind of tragic loss potentially could add depth and precision to his work. Therefore, I had to carefully use myself to facilitate his experience and stay out of the way at the same time.

This is a delicate balance. If I stand too far back and do not use myself as a person with full emotions, I will withhold something precious and powerful from my clients. Simultaneously, I must retain my clinical judgment, skill and reserve so that I can deliver the best possible healing moment. It took me many years and many lessons to master the ability to emote and think at the same time, striking equilibrium between my empathetic self and professional perspective.

When Jack spoke about his mother, it was in rather disparaging tones, as if he were reciting stale words behind which there were no original thoughts—blind truisms. He said she was selfish, heartless, mean and immoral and that she never had loved him or his father. I wondered whether he had introjected beliefs. That is, whether he had swallowed whole someone else's opinions and beliefs about his mother and spoke as if they were from his own experience with his mother, which, of course, he never had. In fact, he had no mature exposure to her. Yet he presented information as if he knew her character. I finally asked him, "How do you know this, Jack?"

The question stunned him, and he replied that those words were his father's version of his mother, and he had always held it to be true. Considering another possibility had never occurred to Jack.

I know all too well how distorted the reports of a rejected spouse can be. After all, in my mother's version, my father was a hopeless alcoholic, a womanizer, a son-of-a-bitch from the day she married him. He was taciturn, impossible to talk to and loved no one but himself, least of all me. Getting love from him was like "getting blood from a stone." It was a classic distortion.

From Jack's story, it was reasonable to inquire whether his father and grandmother, in order to keep his love and loyalty and ensure that they retained custody of him, might have skewed what they told him about his mother. If at all possible, I knew it would be critical for Jack to have his own experience of his mother. I asked him if his mother was still alive and he told me that she was. He'd never attempted to make contact with her, although, when he was 21 years old, he saw her once at a distance at a family funeral.

From his description of her, I assumed that Jack had no capacity to consider the possibility that his mother might really have wanted him and loved him. He was able to experience only his own discomfort at being caught in the crossfire of opposing grownups. I knew we needed to return in time and reenact that moment when Jack stood paralyzed, too young to know his own truth or how to act in his own behalf. This, I hoped, would bring heightened awareness, a new potential for deeper contact with himself and the discovery of a wider range of possibilities regarding his mother and all the people involved in this family split. I also hoped to break the chains that bound him to his identity as the rejected son of his mother, and to let his truth, whatever it might be, come to the foreground.

"Mariah asked me some questions about the reactions of other people involved with the experience I had had when I was 6 years old. She wanted to know who was in the room, what was my mother doing, who was with her, what was my grandmother doing and where were we standing? And what would have been an appropriate behavior of my grandmother?

"We were going to reenact the event the way it happened and then create it the way I wished it would have unfolded. I had seen other people in the workshop reenacting events, so I knew it was coming. I figured, well, okay—and then I experienced a fluttering in my stomach and other bodily nervousness.

"Mariah asked me to choose people in the workshop who would represent people in my family. There was one woman with whom I had connected. I decided she would be my mother. She even looked a bit like I remembered my mother looking at that age. She asked me to pick someone to represent my mother's father, and someone to represent my half-brother, who I think was there as well, but I'm not sure.

"There was a lady in the group I chose to be my grandmother. That was interesting too. She was a heavy-set woman, as was my grandmother. I have an aversion to heavy people, so I needed to choose that woman."

It was time to set the scene. To establish relationships with the people Jack had chosen, I asked him to tell us where various people were standing in his childhood home, and where he was at the time of his mother's attempted reunion. I then placed them in their respective positions and asked Jack what he precisely remembered about the experience. I instructed him to act out the scene in just the way he recalled its happening. There was Jack, clutched tightly by his large, possessive grandmother and flanked by his father while his mother and maternal grandfather asked him if he wanted to come home with them. He stood there, paralyzed and mute, in response to the impossible position of choosing as a 6-year-old. In his silence, he passively and unknowingly clinched the decision to remain in the custody of his grandmother.

When I asked Jack "How are you?" tears softly fell down his face as he whispered, "I'm shocked at how intensely painful this is for me." Now that Jack was open and his emotions available, I wanted to move quickly to create his exact moment of healing. It was time to rewrite history. I then asked Jack what would have been his ideal scenario. He looked perplexed and said that it had never even occurred to him to consider another way.

It's not unusual for traumatic moments to be deeply ingrained in our cells like petrified wood that is locked in time. We rarely entertain other scenarios that potentially could have totally changed the outcome. Or we never consider how, in the present, we have the power to add new dynamics to an old reality, thereby creating a metamorphosis. It took Jack a few minutes to make this leap.

"Instead of my grandmother being the insecure, doting, possessive and jealous person she was and my mother being the fearful, intimidated and insecure person she was, I wish they had been healthy, loving people, who transcended their own wants, needs and desires and put my well-being as a child first.

"Mariah directed the characters to enact this scenario. Instead of my grandmother clutching me, she actually encouraged me to go with my mother instead of staying with her. She gently nudged me toward my mother, who then welcomed me with open arms. I thought that I could never make that walk across the room—my legs felt like lead. My body broke out in a total sweat. I felt that I might pass out. It was a vision that I had never in my entire life even remotely imagined. Mariah helped me make that journey across the room. She instructed me to walk step-by-step, in slow motion, and to be acutely aware of every movement and every breath.

"When I arrived at the other end, there was my mother. She gently put her arms around me. She then sat down, put me

on her lap and rocked me and held me, telling me she loved me and she was so sorry for all her weaknesses. She said that she was here now to protect me, love me and help me grow and that I could have my mother, father and my grandmother too. She whispered in my ear, 'Tell mommy everything, Jack; tell me how it's been for you without me.' As I told her how much I missed her, how scared I was, how sad I was, I was racked with sobs. Words and feelings were pouring out of me that I didn't even know I had. There was music playing—I felt the emotion in it, yet I didn't know what it was. It was all so powerful.

"I remember clearly the feeling of being embraced by that woman—my mother—who was holding me. I felt transported, literally back to being a 6-year-old boy in my mother's arms. The entire room evaporated. Even though I felt the presence of all the people around me, it was such a warm, loving, nurturing feeling being held and rocked. There were even moments when I felt as though I went back to being a baby, an infant, secure and totally taken care of by my mother.

"A moment of skepticism and reservation popped into my mind when I thought, 'What am I doing?' However, a feeling of surrender and relief immediately followed. I was able to let go, relax and take in the warmth, which is something I don't do very often. I've always had, from a young age, a difficult time letting people give me love. I was able to release and let that flow into me."

I had chosen "Lullaby" by Chris Williamson, a song about a mother and her child, which I played twice to give Jack plenty of time to have the complete experience of being held by his mother and to let it sink into his cells. At my instruction, the group had silently and slowly moved in around them, many were crying, some were holding others, and all of us were profoundly moved. As the music came to a close, I asked Jack if he were able to really receive everything he needed from "Mom" in this moment. He confirmed that he was.

What he really had done was open a door that had been closed for his lifetime. He allowed the part of him that was a boy needing mothering to be reowned, felt and provided for. This was a very old and deep wound that needed attention and healing care. Whether or not his real mother was available to him, he needed reparenting. He still needed good mothering. His body needed to feel it.

He also needed to learn to do it for himself whenever the need arose. First, he had to have the experience of what it's like to be held and loved by a good mother. His body, heart and soul needed to experience that. He would have to do some more work therapeutically and would be encouraged to seek out his own mother and test out the reality of history. Then he would need to imagine himself as a good mother for the boy in him, or the man in him, and say over and over the words he longed to hear. This is a process called *reparenting*. He had from his history integrated an abandoning unloving mother. That's the mother he carried within. That mother within needed to transform to a loving, available and emotionally generous mother. He had to be his own mother and provide for himself.

> *"I came to a clear understanding that I was never able to see my mother's side of the story. During the work, I actually felt for the first time, at a bodily level, her turmoil, her problems and her pain. Now I understood something about how she could have done what she did. It wasn't necessarily me she was rejecting as a person and son; rather, it was her own insecurities and inabilities that limited her. I thought now that maybe she did love me, but was too weak to act on that love. She was just as flawed as the rest of us.*

> *"There was a shift. The shift was partly as a result of being able to open up to the possibility that events could have been different. By reenacting that event in the way I would have liked it to occur, at least in my imagination, I could feel the love, the acceptance and openness. That feeling has been gradually growing in me ever since. I was able to grow that feeling of confidence; one of the things that I've*

always lacked is the feeling of confidence in my abilities and my own self."

When his work was over, I encouraged Jack to make a pilgrimage to find his mother or at least find out about her. He seemed frightened and reluctant although he obviously was interested in my suggestion. I offered to meet with him and his mother if that would make the bridge any easier or safer for him.

I knew that Jack needed to discover if his mother were alive or dead and, if possible, to look her in the eyes and find out who she really was instead of the person he imagined her to be for so long.

In the appendix to this book is a letter Jack wrote to me telling of his journey to meet his mother. There is also a letter from his mother to him.

As they weave their familial tapestry and come to terms with their past, Jack and his mother will no doubt go through a challenging process. Some of that process will be painful; much of it will be rich with new-found love and acceptance. What a sacred and heartfelt privilege it is for me to have been a part of their homecoming.

Swallowing Whole

Jack's story is a classic and tragic example of the harm that introjections bring. Small children have no power or ability to discriminate between what is true and what is false. They believe their parents. Certainly Jack did. He believed his father's distorted lie that his mother neither loved nor wanted him. He swallowed it whole and lived as if it were true. He also made major life decisions in that context.

I see this happen often in fractured families. Parents retreat to their own side and then try to divide and conquer the family. Children get caught in the crossfire, controlled by forced introjections. I treated a family in which the mother and father had developed a venomous hatred for each other. Each tried to manipulate the children by demonizing the other parent. The impact on the children was devastating.

Introjection occurs when we are forced or encouraged to swallow whole beliefs or notions that belong to someone else.

Often, we ingest the ideas without thinking about or deliberating their validity or considering the source. We swallow them like liquid, with no chance to spit out what is toxic, and without using our teeth to tear off, chew up and make these ideas our own.

Think about your life. What are the beliefs or attitudes you were encouraged to ingest without question or pause? Have you challenged them? Are there any that are hurting you now? The antidote is to thoroughly chew on/consider/question the ideas, and thoughtfully reject part or all of those that don't match what you really think or feel. Accept what feels right to you. Throw out the rest. Don't be gullible, easy prey or a non-thinking follower. Be aware that, as an adult, you can undo the introjects of your childhood.

The ability to undo introjects in a family will involve getting the story straight about both parents and developing the capacity for listening to opposing viewpoints while carefully sifting through the distortions to find the truth. A sign of maturity and health is the ability to carefully consider conflicting viewpoints, and not take one on as a crusade. Remember, it takes two to tango.

Avoid the destructive call to make a black and white version of the truth; consider all the facts and all the gray areas and polarities of each human being. Oversimplification causes splitting: forming camps of opposing sides with people getting thrown out left and right. Splitting wreaks havoc in families and the world.

Ask yourself, "How much do I see this through my mother's eyes? Do I get caught up in the unhealthy behavior of splitting, where one is out and the other is in?" Fractured families often disown people without careful examination of what really happened. Have you been thrown out or have you thrown someone else out based on an unexamined version of the truth? Do the hard work of seeing the whole picture. Spit out any notions that are not solidly founded or that belong to someone else and have been lodged in you like some foreign body. Arrive at your own opinions based on personal contact and experience and resist being overly influenced by the prejudices or manipulations of others.

Reparenting

You usually introject the styles of parenting from your mother and father. Thus, you become a similar mother to yourself as the mother you had. The same with fathering; if you had a harsh critical father, chances are you will be harsh and critical to yourself at least until you undo the introject you swallowed. Conversely, if your father was warm and supportive, you'll most likely carry on his style of positive regard.

So, whether you know it or not, like Jack, you probably carried into your adult life some behaviors and attitudes of your parents. After all, that's where most of your learned behavior comes from.

You have distinctive ways of being your own inner parents, ways that you think about yourself, give yourself feedback, discipline yourself, protect and take care of yourself. More likely than not you repeat many of the same patterns of your parent's parenting style. As you grew you may have re-examined their style, rejected it and developed your own improved style. Now, if your parents were healthy and well-functioning people with good values and great personal skills, you're one of the lucky ones. You may have reflected upon their value, and consciously made a decision to make their ways your own and continue in their example. However, if you discover you've been poorly mothered or fathered and have learned dysfunctional skills and damaging behaviors that sabotage your life or get in the way of a successful relationship with yourself and others, you will need to reparent yourself.

Reparenting is a process of rejecting unnourishing learned patterns of behavior and re-educating yourself with new skills, beliefs and feelings. This re-education involves looking around at the skills of others and evaluating and selecting which behaviors you want to learn and integrate into your own way of being. Reparenting involves opening up to other sources of mothering and fathering in the world by receiving nourishment from other healthy men and women as well as nature, music, literature and spiritual paths. There are endless sources of parental nourishment. Find and invite people with positive parenting behavior into your life. Learn their skills so that you can treat yourself in the same valuable ways.

If you did not have a good mother, your organism will long for that experience all the days of your life until you respond and provide. If it's not possible to get it from your biological mother, then you must look beyond her to others, and ultimately to yourself, to provide this essential nourishment. Construct a perpetual supply of positive parenting within yourself as well as an inner knowing so that you can always turn to yourself for good mothering if and when you need it. The need for good parenting is vital, even cellular.

We are all our own mothers and fathers. Whether or not we are aware of it, the mother who raised us remains in our self-talk and psychic memory. That's how we mother ourselves. When not in the throes of her alcoholism, my mother was very empathetic. I could go to my mother with anything and know she would care and do whatever she could. So, when I went out on my own, it was relatively easy for me to do this for myself.

I didn't have a father to carry with me, which meant I had to consciously develop a style of fathering. I went out and bought artwork of men with fatherly faces. I enlarged photos of my father and talked to him, imagining myself as my father loving me. I worked at integrating all the good qualities of being my father to carry me and prepare me for choosing a husband and a father for my children.

How are you parenting yourself? Are you protective, comforting, critical, demanding? Are you the first one there to pick yourself up when you fall, or do you abandon yourself in times of need via silence or outright withholding of support?

It's critically important for you to become aware of any ways in which you are carrying on toxic family traditions. Then you must commit yourself to growing past them, thus changing the course of your family history.

Tales of a Wounded Healer

Lost
Stand still. The trees ahead and the bushes beside you
are not lost. Wherever you are is called Here.
And you must treat it as a powerful stranger,
Must ask permission to know it and be known.
The forest breathes. Listen. It answers,
"I have made this place around you,
If you leave it you may come back again, saying Here."

No two trees are the same to the Raven.
No two branches are the same to the Wren.
If what a tree or bush does is lost on you,
You are surely lost. Stand still. The forest knows
where you are. You must let it find you.

—A poem by a Native American elder

Chapter Nine

MOLLY—BREAKING INTO ALIVENESS

Molly, at 5 feet 7 inches with brown curly hair, creamy complexion and big eyes, was an attractive woman in her mid-forties. Born and raised in the west of Ireland, she immigrated to the United States in her early twenties. With effusive warmth and an easy laugh, she gave those around her full attention, in a traditionally Irish feminine way. I met her when she joined the training program as a vehicle for her personal growth and to explore psychotherapy as a potential career change.

Early in the training, she created a very powerful "exact moment of healing," when she addressed the issue of her mother confining her to a sick bed when Molly was a child. Her mother worried and fretted over Molly's health, and was over-protective to the point of undermining her social and emotional development.

"I was raised in an extremely controlled environment in a rural town in Ireland. There was so much worry and care about me because I was the youngest and sickliest of four children. When I was 7 years old, I was given a lung test for tuberculosis in school and the results came back irregular. I didn't actually have tuberculosis, but my mother was terrified that I could catch it, since it was prevalent at that time and our neighbor had recently contracted the disease. I was confined to bed rest for 6 months. Also, shortly before I was born, my brother died of a rare intestinal illness when he was only 16 months old. This left my mother bereft, and terrified of loss.

"I remember feeling so isolated and separated from my siblings and friends. When you're thought to have tuberculosis, you're not allowed near anybody. I was in a room by myself, and saw only my mother, the doctor and my cat.

"When my family went to church, I used to get up and dance on the windowsill. My neighbor would tell on me, because I was supposed to have complete bed rest. No matter what I wanted to do, it was 'You're not strong enough to do that,' or 'You're not tough enough to do that,' or 'If you don't rest, you'll never be healthy.' I was only 7, and didn't feel sick. I wanted to play and I couldn't."

In this work, Molly revealed that the theme of weakness, of not being strong or capable enough to pursue her dreams, had followed her since her childhood. She desperately wanted to break out of a pattern of belittling herself and sabotaging her success. She wanted to neutralize the threat of disaster hanging over her head that she believed was a consequence of moving out on her own behalf. Her conversations with herself had been mimicking those of her mother. Don't move. You're not strong enough. You can't do that. Stay home. Stay safe. Anything could happen. In short, she had internalized the voice of her mother and was effectively continuing to live under her mother's stifling roof.

I found Molly very likeable; she was sweet and possessed that wonderful Irish charm. I also saw a woman, at once obviously capable and confident, and, on the other hand, a bit shy and vulnerable, with great untapped potential.

It is easy for me to see power or the potential for power, in women. I understand the Irish Catholic heritage of being raised in a matriarchal system, but my mother was, in many ways, the opposite of Molly's mother. For as long as I can remember, my mother told me I could do anything, be anything and go as far in life I wanted. Both my mother and my maternal grandmother were powerful woman in the world and certainly in my eyes. They also expected me to excel. If anything, I was given too much power and responsibility at too early an age. When I was 6, my mother would send me out of her office to walk a half-mile to the nearest department store, where I was to purchase my clothes for the season by credit card. I knew the name of the saleswoman and together we would select my clothing. That was normal for me.

As a result of this upbringing, assisting people in self-empowerment comes naturally to me. I assume that people can accomplish their dreams. It's probably one of the things I do best as a professional. Certainly, I had no trouble envisioning Molly as a powerful and accomplished woman. Except for confidence and self-esteem, she had all that it takes. I saw her as personable, intelligent, creative and capable. The only impediment was her past.

> *"When I went up to do my piece of work, I was so nervous. I thought my heart was going to pop out of my body. Mariah helped me recreate that whole scene when I was 7 years old, back in the little cottage that was my home. I selected people in the workshop to represent each of my siblings, my mother and father, even the neighbor. I re-experienced being confined to bed in that tiny room, while my family, as they left for church, said goodbye to me through the door. There I was, again, in my 'prison cell'—not allowed to go with them. I couldn't believe it; the pain and emptiness were just as if I were really back there. I wanted to go to church to see my friends. I wanted to play. Mariah directed the people portraying my parents and siblings to say to me, 'You're too sick; you're not allowed to go. Maybe when you get well. Stay in bed and rest.' How I hated hearing those words again. And they kept saying them over and over. I felt so sad and alone that I began to sob."*

Prior to her explosion into sobbing, there was Molly, sitting on the floor in the workshop, feeling paralyzed and alone and caught between wanting to move and being terrified to move. She was experiencing the same exact feeling she had had in her room in Ireland; if she moved, if she played, if she were free, she might die and break her mother's heart again. Clearly, she was in the "death layer." This is something we all have deep inside, where we feel a void, an emptiness, which we might experience as a kind of death or fear of death or dissolution, where our most intense pain resides. For some people, it shows up as fear of abandonment, loss of love or fear of shattering—breaking into a million pieces. In my own therapy, I remember one of the many times I visited my own death layer and had a dream of a dock with the skeleton of a large fish hanging from a hook. That was it—no people, no sound, no life. The death layer can last a minute, an hour, a week, or for some people going day by day with isolation and pain, for years.

However, the truth is that this emptiness or feelings of nothingness is what Fritz Perls calls a *fertile void*. In this place, you are stripped of all social niceties; all of your roles are gone. All your myriad ways of avoiding your pain and your truth are gone. You are naked and in the thick of it; there are no pretenses. There is nothing but you and your true existence. If you can enter the death layer within yourself with total awareness and support and experience what is hidden there, you can begin to grow and emerge from darkness into light. Then, you can move to a place where you can ex-press (press out) your truth with authentic energy and emotion. You are whole in that moment and truly alive as you enter what I call the *life layer*.

At 45 years old, however, Molly had lived with her prohibitions too long. Her inner knowing created this moment when she had to move—and move she did, into the life layer. It is often very alive and explosive. It is where you make the conscious choice to authentically and fully express your emotions—whether joy, sorrow, fear, anger or sexual intensity. In so doing, you face any conscious or unconscious threat that has inhibited you, and usually find—especially if you have healthy, loving people in your life—that your worst fears are merely vestiges of a former time.

Molly had begun to sob. Authenticity is enlivening.

"Then Mariah offered me the opportunity to design my own ending to the story. What a thrill! I had never even considered that possibility. Naturally, I chose to get up on my windowsill and dance just as I had as a child. Only this time, I decided that all my friends should come into my room to dance with me and encourage me to actually leave the room to go out to play. The people who played my friends literally opened the doors at Pinebrook, the building where the workshop was held. There were beautiful glass French doors that opened onto a huge field covered with wildflowers. It was a perfect dream. They were all saying to me, 'Come on, Molly come out come out. You'll be all right. Come on let's go. It's playtime. Play with us, run, dance.' I was stuck—unable to move. My body felt frozen in time. I kept thinking, 'Is this real? Am I allowed to do this?

Will something bad happen to me?' The leap into motion seemed almost impossible, and yet I wanted so much to break out of this stuckness to go with them. In the end, 40 people in the workshop were yelling to me from the field to come dance and play. It was irresistible, so I finally ran out with them into the field—yelling and twirling and whirling and skipping and laughing and playing with everyone. I had never felt so free in my whole life.

"Mariah blasted some wonderful, fun, dance music and we kept dancing and laughing for what seemed like forever. As I danced, I felt a shift inside of myself as though I were wide open and moving in slow motion."

Molly's experience of doing such profound, personal work in front of so many people had a transforming effect on her. Previously, she had had a tremendous fear, bordering on phobia, of getting up and saying anything in front of a group of people. She couldn't be that open or even conceive of doing what she had just done. Now, she had a different belief system about her capabilities and herself.

"The message is that I can trust and put myself more into what I want to do. I can choose not to listen to the force of the voices telling me, 'You can't do that.' I need to trust in myself, that yes, I can do this, even though the forces are saying, 'I'm going to stop you.' I can trust in myself and believe in my ability to overcome that. My own inner force is making me stronger."

A while later I asked Molly, in a private session, how she was feeling following her work. I noticed that her posture was particularly erect, and her eye contact very strong. In looking back, Molly reflected on the contrast between herself before and after her work.

"In the moments following the work, when I was driving home and the next day, I was able to experience a self-assurance that I never had before. I thought to myself,

'Maybe this is who I am now.' I don't have the right words for the feeling of relief. It was a whole new awareness and something that I truly wanted to believe about myself. I didn't want to be afraid any longer that people would dislike me if I had self-confidence. I wasn't feeling great or boastful; it just simply felt real to me."

For a long time, Molly had felt out of control. Through this work, she had gained confidence in who she was and what she could do, beyond what others told her she could do, which was very little. She used to put everyone on a pedestal, and put herself on the ground. Everyone was better than she was, and she didn't see any faults or weaknesses in them. This was a feeling she had had in every part of her life: her work, her family, everything. Through this process, Molly learned to put herself on the pedestal and to be parallel with other people. She learned that she, too, had greatness.

Claiming Your Authentic Voice

Like Jack in the last chapter, Molly's work demonstrates the power of introjection and how it can dominate and damage your life until you undo it and develop your own authentic self-supporting voice. Remember, introjection occurs when you swallow whole messages from outside yourself, without chewing on them first, and they become what you believe. Molly swallowed, without question or attempt at refusal, the belief that she was weak and not as strong as other people. She was too young to filter her mother's words, sift out the truth and discard the useless, toxic aspects of what her mother said.

A more mature person might have questioned the facts, while considering her mother's concerns; spitting out the poison and retaining what was valuable. Children cannot discriminate. They usually introject.

The work of healing in a case like this involves figuratively vomiting up your corrosive introjects and replacing them with your own well-considered, thoroughly chewed beliefs. The idea is that when presented with a new idea, you:

Chew on it (think about it, compare it, question it, research it).

Spit out what you don't like (what you consider untrue, not applicable, perhaps toxic).

Swallow (claim as your own) what you believe to be true.

The Four Steps

I went on to teach Molly some effective tools for developing and deepening her relationship with herself. In Robin's story, I described how it is most effective to take these steps while looking at yourself in a mirror. Don't judge how you look but instead really see yourself as a person with whom you want to connect. Here's what I told Molly:

Look into your own eyes. Breathe and ask what you are feeling now. Use your own first name. Wait for the answers from the person in the mirror.

Ask yourself what you want or need about that feeling or need. Again become that person in the mirror and share what you want or need.

Return to the position of provider/inquirer and provide a creative response to what you want or need. For instance, if you have been feeling lonely and needing love, then as the provider you say something like, "I hear you are wanting love and appreciation, and I want you to know I'm fully with you now. You are not alone. You are with me. I do love you and I am committed to a path of learning to love you even more."

Switch and be the receiver. Working with your breath, inhale, and visualize the love you have been given by yourself, absorbing it into every fiber of your being.

After a lot of practice in these four steps, you'll be able to do it efficiently and effectively wherever you are. Practice until it becomes an automatic knee-jerk reaction, integrated into the way you live with you. Again, the four steps are:

What do I feel?
What do I want or need?
Provide.
Receive.

This is a practical intrapersonal use of the Awareness and Contact Cycle discussed in Chapter Two. If you master it, this skill alone will change the course of your life. It will help you keep balanced, stay full and arrive anywhere already loved.

Tales of a Wounded Healer

One day we shall sit together
in the rain
on the wet green grass
and watch how earth receives.

—From a poem by Mariah Fenton Gladis, 1972

Chapter Ten

LISA—COME, LET ME LOVE YOU

Lisa's impressive physical appearance did not match her reticent personality. She was tall, about 5 feet 9 inches, and large-framed. Her complexion was soft and creamy, with blonde hair, striking blue eyes and a warm, endearing smile that drew me to her. Even though she was a 29-year-old woman, she was as shy as a young child. This self-consciousness limited her interaction with her classmates in our 3-year training program and kept her from initiating any personal contact with me. She spoke very little, and when she did, I could hardly hear her. I would later understand that self-doubt held her back; she didn't feel worthy of my attention.

For the first year, Lisa tended to hang out with a woman friend whom she knew prior to the training. Although not an initiator, her response in any interaction with others was always kind and friendly. When classmates did hot seat work, Lisa willingly participated, and extended her full attention. She displayed extraordinary compassion for their pain.

As I continued working with Lisa, I observed a chronic, extreme vulnerability that made the world an unsafe place for her and she a helpless victim in it. It was obvious that she had not developed her own sense of power, confidence and value. A sense of scarcity, compounded by low self-esteem, left her feeling she was not worthy enough to have more than a little of anything in life. That powerlessness showed itself in several ways. She cried a lot. The tears, stemming from deep identification with sorrow and fear, didn't function as a healthy release or comfort. Lisa, like many of us, had not learned to respect and respond lovingly to her own tears. She cried into a vacuum rather than into her own embrace and self-love. My healing strategy for her needed to include highly focused training in how to support, feel compassion for and empower herself.

She was so blinded by her programming that she couldn't allow in the love and acceptance that surrounded her in the group. She was literally starved for emotional sustenance and nurturing with no ability to receive or contain the positive affection that was coming her way. Stuck in the quicksand of depression, scarcity and isolation, she cried most of the time. She felt no lasting relief from the pain, even if she, momentarily, let one of us care for her. Her system was like a colander—whatever love went in, fell out. Nothing was distributed and retained throughout her organism.

Music served as an occasional oasis for Lisa. She enjoyed singing and playing the guitar, although mostly for herself. It was difficult for her to perform in public. On one occasion, however, she sang for the group. Even though she had a lovely voice, I knew that inside her, there was a bigger, stronger voice longing to be released.

People who are shy and self-conscious like Lisa, often unknowingly, turn their aggression back against themselves, instead of using it to make contact in the world. They then become their own targets for self-criticism, which leads to chronic depression. I knew I needed to activate Lisa's lost aggression, which she had turned against herself. Whenever someone lives as a martyr or victim, there is always an aggressive polarity that has been disowned or amputated preventing the person from being whole. This disowned aggressive self needs to emerge and be renowned in order for the client to become whole and achieve a healthy balance.

Let's consider aggression in terms of eating food, a simple everyday act we do unconsciously. Let's slow down the process to examine it. As you put food in your mouth, it becomes necessary to chew it, to break it down so that it can be assimilated into your organism. Your teeth "de-structure" or destroy your food. When you chew, you destroy. However, this destruction is a healthy form of aggression. A chunk of carrot is mutilated to mush and liquid so that your body can swallow and digest its nutrients. It's the same for living. You must be able to make contact and figuratively chew what you are meeting in the environment so that it can be properly assimilated.

If someone presents you with an idea, you need to have the discriminating capability to "chew" on the idea: you thoroughly examine it, break it down and decide what you like about it and what you don't. Swallow the best and spit out the rest. Too many people treat their environment as a liquid and swallow things whole without intelligent consideration and selectivity.

So aggression is not simply anger, it's also a healthy antidote to passivity. It provides the capacity to meet successfully with any stimulus in your environment, whether people, food or ideas. Aggression, in its most positive function, is equal to power and intelligent contact in the world. Without access to it, you are doomed to live a passive, ineffectual, un-nurtured life.

The purpose for working on your anger is so that you can complete unfinished business, including unexpressed resentment, unfair treatment and jealousy. Clearing a path to your own capacity for assertiveness, power and the ability to disagree and speak the truth at all times, is pertinent to recovery. Setting boundaries—developing the ability to know when and how to say "no"—is just as important. I work to get clients in touch with their anger and to provide a safe environment so that they can express themselves freely and in full measure, while unblocking dormant energies.

Early in the training program, Lisa remained paralyzed whenever I would challenge her to express opinions or reasonable demands or to voice resentment or anger. Yet I knew she was working hard within herself. She was an excellent student who would read and absorb the material and hand in assignments in a timely and accomplished manner.

It was hard to get Lisa started; she was afraid of expressing her anger. Once she crossed through the barrier, however, tremendous potential became available to her. Lisa's discovery of her aggression began on a day she addressed an issue about an older sibling by whom she felt dominated and rendered powerless. After much encouragement from the group and while I positioned her body—standing, legs balanced and flexed, back straight to support her, shoulders back and chest widened, head upright taking a full breath—Lisa was able, for the first time, to release a loud, enraged voice. She screamed out to her visualized sibling some expletives and other words such as, "How dare you!" and "Don't you ever, ever, ever, do that again!"

Immediately following her outburst, Lisa unleashed a spontaneous burst of laughter. She asked, "Was that me? I just can't believe it was me. I didn't know I had that in me."

Once she had re-owned her aggression and was capable of meeting her experiences with health and the capacity to break them down and chew on them, the next step for Lisa was to develop her capacity for receptivity. She had learned to figuratively bite and chew on her experiences, and to express her thoughts and feelings clearly and energetically. She could now move out on her own behalf. Next, she needed to learn to receive, assimilate and integrate what she was being given—love, information, touch, contact—for her own health and nourishment.

The nature of receptivity is not commonly understood in our culture. It is an action and an art that must be methodically learned. The essential foundation of being loved is first to love yourself. This prepares your internal environment to allow love from the outside to enter. Then the love comes your way. You need to stop, look and be aware that love is being offered as a precious gift. You need to inhale deeply, purposefully permitting love to enter your body. Ideally, every pore of your body becomes a sponge, soaking up the offering. Finally, when love is offered, you must develop the capacity to contain and hold onto that love.

This transformation takes concentration, awareness and purposeful action. The length of time it takes people to learn receptivity depends on their history and the extent of present-day blockages and unfinished business from their past. It takes a courageous person to go through all of this to get to the other side, the receptive state.

Two years of hard work in the training program prepared Lisa to take a giant step. I designed an experiment on receptivity and containment for her that would shift her in a profound and lasting way. She writes about the experience as well as I could describe it. Therefore, I will let her words stand on their own. I believe that her story has a universal quality that speaks to many of us.

"The exact moment my healing began was on November 18, 1995. If I were looking at the 'bigger picture,' I would have to nod my head and admit that I had been in therapy for depression. Certainly, these attempts to find healing served as the background and foundation for the singular event that began my transformation.

"The place of my healing moment was Pinebrook, where I was attending a weekend workshop. This particular weekend was a requirement of my second year training. The

program expects its students to learn through experience, the assumption being that a therapist can only facilitate healing in others to the extent that he or she has experienced healing in himself or herself. At this point, I had been counseling survivors of sexual abuse for 3 or 4 years, and had wanted to further my therapeutic abilities as well as experience my own personal growth.

"My past is as similar and as unique as that of any client who finds his or her way to Pinebrook. My family had its share of dysfunction and love. My mother was overwhelmed by her life and could not meet the needs of her 3 children, so her love often took the form of criticism. My father distanced himself emotionally from the chaos of our home; his love was generally out of my reach. My older sister acted out her frustrations by becoming physically violent toward me. I coped with my life by withdrawing in a fashion similar to my father's. My withdrawal eventually took on the aspects of clinical depression. Other events in my life solidified my fear of people. As a child, I was subjected to torment and humiliation by my peers; as a young adult, I was raped after a party at a campus fraternity.

"My experiences taught me some hard lessons. I believed that I was not as acceptable as everyone else, that my body was an appropriate target for violence, and that those who should protect me would not. With all the strength I could muster, I adapted to these lessons and let them shape my identity. I learned to exist alone in the world. I decided that I would not subject myself to the pain of rejection, and so I numbed myself to my desire for interaction. Out of habit and hyper-vigilance, I saw only the potential for sorrow. I built a stone wall around my heart so that I would be well defended. And I kept these measures a secret from everyone, especially myself.

"As a student of Mariah's, I saw how my experiences had led me to cut myself off from the cycle of feeling and responding to myself. This was not a huge revelation. I already understood that my experiences in childhood had hurt me. I could talk at length about why I had become the person I was. Soon, I was presented with the philosophy of personal responsibility. I was asked to believe that I was responsible for the life I was leading. I was asked to believe that I could choose to make my life and myself different. Awareness wasn't enough; I had to take action.

"All my life, my fears had protected me from exactly this. Mariah told me, 'Yes you can, you already know how, of course you are good enough, and you've known it all along.' So I found myself at a weekend workshop, watching other people take the risks they needed to take to get on with their lives. I wanted that for myself. I signed up for a workspace.

"I found myself in the middle of my worst nightmare. I was in the 'hot seat,' and 25 people were looking at me, wishing me well. Some were people I had grown to know and care about; some were relative strangers. Some had already sat in the chair I now occupied and they had spoken about their pain and their needs, and they had received love and healing. One person, in particular, a woman named Virginia, had offered me her love and friendship over the course of the previous year, and I had responded with tentative and often ambiguous gestures. I wanted her friendship yet I had pushed her away. Other people from my class who had reached out to me at one time or another were there. Catie, Rob, Marcie, Ann, Nancy. Sitting there, surrounded by safe and loving people, I felt completely alone.

"Mariah asked me, 'What do you need?' I knew what my work was. I had to find out how to receive the love that these people were offering me. I told her that I knew, I understood, that I was lovable, but I never felt loved. I knew that Virginia cared about me, yet I felt completely disconnected from her. I was afraid to talk about this; I was afraid Virginia would give up on me once she realized her *gifts were going to waste. I described my experience of being loved, of knowing that it was around me, surrounding me, and feeling it wash over me without ever penetrating me, like a shadow, like water running off a duck's back. I told her that I always felt empty inside, hollow. Mariah asked me to choose someone from whom I would like to receive love. I chose Virginia. She was given a bouquet of flowers to symbolize her love and friendship. She extended this gift to me; my job was to go to her and to receive it. As I prepared myself, Mariah said to me, 'Remember that receiving is an activity—you must work at it.'*

"*I became very confused. This was a new concept to me, receiving as an action. I was aware that giving was active, but I always thought that the receiver was passive, that showing up was the most a person had to do. I walked up to Virginia and she held out the bouquet. I was aware that she was very still, just standing there with these flowers in her hand, expecting me to—what? To take the flowers? I didn't deserve this beautiful gift. I had let her down so many times. Who was I to take anything from her? I was too much trouble to have as a friend. I was too needy and demanding. I wanted to apologize to her for making her go through so much. I wanted to tell her to stop trying because I didn't want to disappoint her any more than I had already.*

"*I think she spoke to me, told me how much she valued me, how much she wanted me in her life. I was appalled that she would have such a feeling for me. How could I ever live up to her expectations? How could I ever be as good to her as she was to me? I was crying tears of longing as I replied that I wanted to be her friend, I wanted to be a good friend. Still, I didn't know what to do. I took the flowers from her, but they were only flowers, pretty and impassive. I said, 'Thank you,' a polite gesture that sounded more like a question than a statement. I was more alone than ever. I had failed. I felt total despair as I turned my back on Virginia to tell Mariah that I couldn't do it, I was not feeling* anything go in, I was not receiving this beautiful gift Virginia had given me. I felt the presence of an invisible wall separating us. Nothing could penetrate the thickness of this wall from either side, not even love.

"I felt sure that my time was up, that Mariah would shrug her shoulders and tell me to come back to another weekend and try again. I returned to the chair beside her, waiting for her to speak kind words of next time. Instead, she instructed the entire group to stand in a circle, she told me to stand in the center. She told the group to shower me with love, to put their hands and bodies into it, to pour the abundance of their love over me. And she told me to take it in, to go to each person and take the gift they were offering and to put it inside me. I used my hands, trying to pluck out of thin air the substance of the love that seemed determined to elude my grasp.

"I heard music playing; an instrumental version of John Denver's 'Annie's Song.' I sang the words in my head, 'You fill up my senses, like a night in the forest, like the mountains in springtime, like a walk in the rain.' Mariah told me to see love in front of me, to place it inside of me, to be an active receiver. I envisioned myself grasping raindrops with both hands, and placing them in a wicker basket that I wore against my body. I saw the raindrops seep through and drain onto the floor. As I went from person to person, I berated myself for doing it wrong, for looking like a fool. Was I spending too much time trying with each person? Too little time? I felt panicked and desperate as I attempted to hoard these drops of rain/love in my basket. I came to Virginia and saw the tears in her eyes as I fell deeper and deeper into frustration and despair.

"I was more than halfway around the circle. The music had stopped and started again. I was terrified; I was angry; I was trying so hard. Pluck the drop from the air, put it in the basket, again, again. I felt greedy and small and very tired. The room seemed dark and I felt like I had tunnel vision. I was hunched over my imaginary basket and I felt closed in upon myself, claustrophobic. I looked up and saw Catie in front of me, tall and solid. She was wearing pink; her eyes found my eyes and I stopped. I planted my feet into the floor. I took a deep breath, aware that my breathing had become very shallow. I was no longer aware of my thoughts, only of the need to stop racing and hoarding and grasping and gasping for breath.

"I was fighting for my life and I was fighting both sides of the battle. A newly awakened part of myself was fighting for the right to love and be loved. To do that, I had to challenge my survivor; the part of myself that had built the wall that had protected my heart since I was a child. I wanted to be connected to my loving friends and to do that I had to break through my wall. At that instant, as my eyes met Catie's, I realized that I couldn't be both protected from contact and loved. I couldn't hoard drops of love in some container, to be taken out and felt when I was safely alone. I had to surrender.

"I threw my arms out wide, stretching and opening my hands and my chest and lungs and I felt something within me crack. I felt something behind or within or around my breastbone, over my heart, snap into pieces. I heard the sound of ice breaking on a melting lake. My head was tilted back and I could breath. I could feel a connection with myself and with every person in the room and I could feel rivers of love flowing through a crack in my armor, flowing into the hollow, empty space inside of me. The music was still playing 'come let me love you, come love me again.' I felt terrified and comforted, energized and alive, connected and safe.

"It lasted for seconds, and it has lasted forever. I could not tolerate this new sensation, but I wanted to be held and cradled. I wanted to give thanks. I wanted to stop it. I wanted to be reassured that it would never end. I burst into tears, loud, deep sobs that wracked my entire body. I ran to

Mariah, who was like a mother to me, my savior. I hugged her to thank her for this gift, and she whispered words of comfort and encouragement in my ear. I turned to Mark to be held in his solid embrace and took in his warmth and support. I turned to Dori and to the others in the group. I hugged Catie, and I could feel her presence within me. Virginia hugged me and I took in the gift of her arms and her love.

"That was over a year ago. I am told by others that it was as memorable a moment for them as it was for me. I returned to the training program and my therapist with renewed faith in the power of love as a healing force, in the power of my own ability to heal. I was frightened that the feeling would not last, that days or weeks later I would again be numb and unresponsive. I was afraid that I had not sustained the moment long enough to truly benefit from the work.

"So far, my fears have been unfounded. My relationship with Virginia has blossomed into a deep friendship. I no longer push her away when she offers her love to me. I feel more available to others, and I have been told that I am perceived as being more present. The wall still exists, but I have built a doorway through which love and light pour into my being.

"I have spent many days still feeling depressed. There are times when I feel hopeless. Each time I find my way out, sometimes with the help of my therapist, more and more often through writing in my journal or simply taking time out to be with myself. I have experienced many more healing moments with Mariah and members of my class, and I plan on experiencing more. I trace all of these moments to their source in the moment I discovered how to receive; for this was the moment I learned the fundamentals of giving. As I experienced the vital energy of the act of receiving, I learned that I am a part of this world, connected to the energies of the universe. I learned to exist

*in a world filled with an abundance of love. Each day I take
in this lesson anew."*

The Gift of Receptivity

Like parched earth, when your soil has been deprived of water
and nourishment, your surface becomes hard and solidified, making
you difficult to penetrate. It is not as simple as it seems, this art of
receiving, especially when old wounds have us covered in armor or a
crust. Your soil needs to be prepared, tilled, turned over and
reconstructed so that it is pervious to sustenance. Letting go of an
outer casement can be very threatening. It means a whole
reconfiguration of that which you have used to protect you.
Perhaps, early in life when you hardened yourself, it did protect you
by keeping hurtful, toxic energy out. But, if you've lived encased
year after year, you begin to dry up and starve. Now, the key thing
that once protected you, could destroy you; it can starve you of
relationships and heart-and-soul exchanges with other people.

Have you ever been given a gift and not really received it? Do
you know how you resist receiving? Do you deny the love as
genuine? Do you devalue the giver? Do you clench your body
behind an outer shell? Do you hardly notice what you've been
given? Do you overlook it, or take it for granted, or actively push
it away and refuse it? Or do you remember a time when you did fully
receive someone's offering? By that I mean, noticed the gift and
the giver?

Lisa had been dried up, shrinking, becoming less of who she was,
and no longer growing. She had to receive nourishment from outside
herself in order to blossom into full life. To have her first
experience of full receptivity, I knew she had to become fully aware
of her body's armor so that she could release it. She also had to
move. So I asked her to stand in the middle of the group. Initially
she rotated her shoulders inward, pulling back her chest and heart. I
asked her to shift her body and stand straight, feeling her spine
supporting her. With her shoulders aligned and leading with her
heart, I asked her to move to the music while she slowly and with
deep concentration opened her arms and hands for the purpose of
letting in all the love coming toward her. It was what is called a
satori, a spiritual and emotional waking up, a moment of

enlightenment with each breath. As she absorbed her gifts and experienced true receiving for the first time in her life, she became more and more alive. Her tears now were tears of joy and excitement.

How well do you receive the love of the closest persons in your life? Receiving is an action, an activity requiring concentration and purposeful movement. How much do you take in? Rate yourself from zero to 100%. If your number is low, you have discovered a powerful tool to change the quality of your life. You have the need and the opportunity to receive all the time; from nature, loved ones, books, music, food, through a galaxy of moments in your life. You need to maximize the moments; see the gift and the giver. Be in full contact and open up.

Notice your body. Work with your breath. Inhale the love all the way down to your toes. Imagine it filling you up. Hold onto it. Don't be a colander by letting it come in one side and fall out the other. Retain the sweetness of the moment in your forever place. If you don't have a forever place in your body, design and develop one; it is a place you can return to at any moment when you need love and nourishment. Love won't enter you unless you allow it in. Invite it in. Take it in. Don't be a brick wall. Don't be impervious. Turn your body into a sponge. Let love saturate every cell. Visualize it. Inhale. Receive.

Think about what went into the gift giving: the effort, the thought, the generosity and the well wishes of the giver. Take time and inhale. Let the gift and the spirit in which it was given enter deep inside. Let it touch your heart. As you do, you will naturally overflow with appreciation for the giver.

Remember, receiving well is a powerful gift to the giver. Lisa's openness nourished the whole circle of givers. By your receptivity, you make it a win-win situation and well worth the effort for the giver to have directed and delivered his or her love to you. Express your full appreciation. Allow your hearts to touch and realize the sweet specialness of the moment. Use your eyes to really see the gift and the giver. Hear the words. Be in full contact and gratefulness, the natural outgrowth of receptivity. Allow yourself to be moved. Soft. Pliable. The precise sensation of deep appreciation is one of the greatest pleasures we can feel in this lifetime. Enjoy it.

Tales of a Wounded Healer

History, despite its wrenching pain, cannot be unlived,
but if faced with courage, need not be lived again.

—Maya Angelou

Chapter Eleven

MARISA—UNRAVELING FAMILY SECRETS

"When I was 5 years old, a cousin 4 years older than I began sexually abusing me. The abuse happened intermittently at my parents' house, his house, and other times we would see each other. He was good friends with my brother, so I kept it a secret; I didn't want to 'rock the boat.' The last time it happened was at my parents' house on New Year's Eve, several years after it had started. Everybody was at the house—my parents, his parents, all my family, and all the kids. We were downstairs playing pool. My brother ran up the stairs and said something like, 'The last one up...' leaving my cousin and I alone.

"My cousin threw me on the bed. I was kicking; he was touching me all over. I remember intensely wanting to get away from him, but not wanting to scream. I did get away and ran upstairs. That's the last time it happened. I don't know why it was the last time, it just was. I was 12.

"I have painful memories of those abuses. I think the reason why I went through it without telling anyone was because he would threaten that if I did, he would "go after" my twin sister. Since I was always considered the strong twin and she was labeled the weak one, I wanted to protect her.

"About that time, my father started to drink and my parents were always fighting, threatening each other with divorce. It was hard for my sister and me to live in that house. It was chaos. We felt alone. My older brother was off doing his own thing, getting ready for college. My other brother and sister were living on their own. My sister and I were the only ones left at home, and we had no idea what was going on.

"My father was a war veteran whose plane had been shot down during the Second World War. Because of that experience, he had all this post-traumatic stress and he would constantly drink and get very violent. He would scream and yell and have his guns out and threaten to kill himself and us. We were sure he would some day.

"He never physically touched us but he would yell in our faces and chase my mom around, knocking down doors and being verbally abusive. We were trapped in our own home with this behavior. It was the focus of our daily lives and I won't ever forget it."

Marisa's history was full of chronic, long-term abuse and family dysfunction, which more than likely contributed to her diagnoses of autoimmune diseases. When trauma repetitively occurs over time, it almost always affects the body, heart, mind and soul and demands a multi-faceted course of healing, which usually takes longer than treating a single-event trauma. It requires multiple exact moments of healing. Chronic trauma often is more deeply embedded in the personality; the remnants of it seem to hide in the recesses of the organism. In order to ensure her safety and full recovery, I had to be thorough in my work with Marisa. Let me share more of her history with you, so that you can understand what she was up against and how she had to make monumental decisions so that, in her mind, she could protect her sister and family.

Another issue Marisa had to deal with was that her father was well known in the community. Away from the home, he certainly cared about his work and always did a great job. But when he returned home, it was another story. That's when he turned into a maniac, yelling and screaming and fighting with her mother. It was really difficult for Marisa to keep this secret from the rest of the world. And yet she did. Worse still, her mother would never blame her father, and would leave the kids alone, sometimes going away for days at a time.

It was craziness, a very tough time, and sad in many ways. I think what helped Marisa was having a twin and a bonded family even though it was dysfunctional. Once her brothers knew what she was going through, they were very protective; she felt especially supported by them.

Marisa could not escape the damage, even with the support of friends and siblings. Much of her stress lodged in her body, which is not unusual for people with a history such as hers, especially when they are forced to harbor secrets for a long time. In my experience, I have seen many women with family histories of addiction and/or sexual abuse develop serious eating disorders whether it be anorexia, bulimia or obesity. They also can develop serious illness early in life. Marisa manifested both illness and an eating disorder. Between undergraduate and graduate school Marisa went home for about 9 months. With all the craziness surrounding this type of home life, she had a bout of anorexia and lost more then 40 pounds.

> *"I had physical signs—the eating disorder, losing all that weight and being anorexic for a period of time. I didn't have control of anything in my life back then and I was living at home. It was self-abusive and very dangerous. I remember back then not being alive, not being awake. I was running 6 to 10 miles a day. I can't believe I didn't pass out or land in the hospital. There were real physical problems. I didn't get my period for 9 months. I mean, the light was on but nobody was home. I was functioning, doing what I had to do. In graduate school, I was in relationships that were not healthy for me at all. I chose men who didn't like women."*

Marisa's healing journey started in her early twenties when she began psychotherapy. A few years later, she came to me. Tall, at 5 feet 10 inches, with light skin and medium brown, shoulder-length hair, she had a remarkable presence, a combination of strength and vulnerability. Through a blend of individual and group therapy, we addressed many of her issues of twinship, being the child of an alcoholic father and sexual abuse. She was a joy to work with, extremely self-motivated and bright. She had the courage to do everything she needed to do to heal.

One of her first and most vital exact moments of healing occurred when Marisa courageously faced her sexual abuse through a simulated confrontation with her abuser. That work enabled her to follow up with literally addressing him in life and revealing to her family the secret she had kept for more than 20 years.

"I remember one workshop, when I was addressing my sexual abuse, Mariah asked me what I remembered had happened and what I would now want to happen if I could re-write history. I knew immediately. I wanted justice. We created a court scene where I got to be the prosecutor and tell my story in detail—speaking aloud the crime and things that my cousin did to me. I chose participants from the workshop to be on the jury and they sentenced him with castration. The judge slammed down the gavel, pronouncing him guilty as charged and the workshop police rushed in and roughly escorted him off to jail. I loved that. It was perfect!

"That was compelling, especially since the people playing the parts were friends of mine. It was really good for me, very empowering. That experience was early in my therapy. Back then I was timid and scared. I felt like a powerless victim, since I perceived that my perpetrator had all the power. Other people in the group were able to be angrier than I. I felt like a child being pushed along by their example and words and Mariah's guidance.

"However, during this experience, I remember starting in a place of powerlessness, then moving through that to becoming really angry. In my old pattern, I got stuck in feelings of helplessness and keeping the secret about my abuse. A lot of my life was stuck there, which was very damaging to me physically and emotionally and kept me closed off from people. This time, for the first time, I felt true personal power.

"I remember feeling scared and powerless at the beginning. He had all the power. Going into that place of being scared and powerless and moving through that and getting angry: hitting a mattress with a bat, screaming and yelling and getting that out. Then being rescued, nurtured and getting help. That was really important because one of the themes

for me was that if you are really strong, you don't need anyone. I've always had a resistance to receiving, whether it was verbal or physical."

Marisa had multiple sources contributing to feelings of helplessness and victimization: the abuse, the inability to change her father, her mother's role model as a female victim with a male abuser. It was critical to provide Marisa with more experiences that would empower her and help her to direct her healthy aggression outward instead of inward. During this time, she took an important step.

"I wrote my cousin a letter in which I was very clear and told him what I remembered him doing to me, how it affected my life. I wanted him to know that if I ever found out that he'd hurt anyone else, especially his daughters, I'd step forward to protect them. He began calling people, members of my family, his parents, and saying that I was sick. Then I told my mom the whole story. She went for a long walk—she felt a lot of guilt. He was my father's brother's son.

"Keeping the secret had made me rigid and in my own little world. There wasn't a lot of contact going on. I could control my own little world. I was fine. I lived in a small apartment in a barn and I lived my life and it seemed happy. I was working with sexual abuse survivors and victims of all sorts of crimes. Through that work a lot of my stuff started coming up. That's when I started going to Adult Children of Alcoholics meetings. And I saw one therapist at that time who said to me, 'You are the sickest person I have ever met.' She told me there was no hope."

Marisa continued to work in several sessions on her sexual abuse scenes. She directly expressed her rage at a person playing the role of her perpetrator, physically overpowering him and then being rescued and nurtured by people who cared about her and who arranged for the help that she needed. It was necessary to train her to receive help since she had formed a counter-dependent attitude of false bravado, "I can take care of myself, I don't need anyone." She had to accept her own healthy need for capable people who would provide for her as she gradually became more and more open, and willing to be vulnerable and authentic with her feelings.

In her ongoing therapy group, there was a man who disclosed that he had abused someone in his family. He was someone she had come to deeply respect and care for, so his admission was an intense and surprisingly wonderful moment for her. She had labeled all abusers, especially because of the work she was doing with sexual abuse survivors, as evil men whom she hated. Here was someone she really loved who was saying, 'I did this.' At the same time, he expressed feelings of guilt and shame. The ability to see him as a person and actually feel compassion for him was one of her most healing moments. She listened to the conditions of his home life, which certainly didn't excuse what he'd done, but his story helped her see him in a different light and begin to understand the pain he was carrying. This prepared her to address her issues regarding men. She had gone from a place of hating men, to a place of knowing that she could live the rest of her life imagining that all men were abusers or alcoholics. Now she saw that she had another choice. She could do the critical work needed to make her peace with men, to learn to differentiate between healthy and unhealthy men and to be able to invite and incorporate healthy men into her life. Her decision to work on her issues with men was a crucial turning point for her.

Marisa had come a long way and was now a strong, compassionate and expressive woman. Yet, I felt she was still vulnerable to recreating childhood trauma in her adult life. For example, the man she had been seeing for a number of years was clearly an alcoholic. He had reneged on a number of promises, including marriage, and yet she was unable to break away from him.

She initiated her next piece of work, and asked me to push her hard, because she really needed to make headway in transforming her relationships with men to a healthier level. I knew she could handle whatever awarenesses might come to her. So I lined up the men in the workshop in front of her and said to Marisa, "Who are they to you? What do you imagine about them? What do you think about them that you have not said aloud?" True to her character, Marisa was very forthcoming, admitting that she had transferred onto them qualities that belonged to her father and the cousin who had sexually abused her.

"Mariah directed me to choose 6 men in the workshop and have them stand in a line in front of me. Then she asked me to go up to each man and look at him in the eyes and say the truth about what my private suspicions were. I said, 'This is what I imagine about you. You are an abuser. You are violent. And you are an addict.' Of course, these were men I knew, some of them very well. It was difficult saying this to them one-by-one, and yet it was true about me. That was my secret suspicion of all men."

I then played the song "Desperado" to emphasize for Marisa awareness of how she was keeping herself separate and alone. "Desperado, why don't you come to your senses? You've been out mending fences for so long now. Oh, you're a hard one but I know that you've got your reasons. These things that are pleasing you, can hurt you somehow."

"Mariah had the men circle around me and she asked me to position my body, to sculpt myself in a way that expressed how I protect myself from men. I stood with my arms up and my hands pushing them away. My chest was caved in; my legs were readied for fight or flight. She had me really exaggerate the stance and concentrate on feeling it. I heard the words to the song and had a flood of awareness about how I isolate myself, while simultaneously feeling fear and longing.

"Mariah then directed me to be silent as the men gave me feedback about the way they experienced me. Each used various words, yet essentially said the same thing—that I was defensive, not verbally, but physically. Hearing that was really hard, especially since I had to just listen and not respond.

"Mariah asked me to get down on my knees in front of each man, look him in the eye and say, 'You are not an abuser or

an alcoholic. You are not any of these things. You are a person. You are valuable. I'm sorry that I put my judgments onto you and have not seen you clearly.' I was actually honoring men for the first time, and sobbing. This was so difficult and emotional for me to do, yet important for my personal healing. I'll never forget that moment."

As Marisa revealed the intensity and pervasiveness of her transference of the destructive characteristics of her father and cousin onto all men, it became clear to me that she most likely had not had experiences of safe contact with men, other than her brothers, whose value she could see without the interference of contaminated remnants of her history. It was as if she were wearing a black veil that discolored what she saw. I wanted to provide an experience of lifting the veil so that her heart could come out from undercover and see possibilities again. She had harbored many secrets for a long time and essentially lived in isolation from men: the secret of abuse in the family, the secret of her eating disorder, the secret of her deep mistrust and judgments of all men. She needed to be safe enough to self-reveal, and have a positive experience with men. Although her resistance to contact served to protect her in the past, and may have saved her life, it no longer served her in the present.

Essentially, an exact moment of healing was called for; one where she could take responsibility, apologize for her behavior, and give honoring where it was due. The six men were to stand in for innocent, non-abusive, albeit imperfect, men, whom Marisa had silently accused. Marisa had done enough effective confrontational work with abusive men. Now it was time to stop globalizing her accusations and to differentiate between abusers and healthy men. In short, she needed to open her heart to good men.

She was in a repetitive pattern of unclear, unsound contact that needed deconstruction and reconstruction. She needed to see that her rage was not with all men; it was with very specific men and had to be contained and delivered where it belonged, thereby freeing her up for clear and healthy contact with carefully chosen men.

So why did I bring her to her knees? As I've said before, I believe that as you are hurt by experience, so do you heal by experience. The act of kneeling, at its most sacred meaning, expresses giving honor and respect—think prayer or a marriage proposal. It can also express a deep apology to another, and can imply asking for understanding, forgiveness and a blessing. In this context, it certainly did not, in any way, imply submission, humiliation or self-deprecation.

In Marisa's case, her body had taken the hits of all the trauma and she needed healing on a physical level as well as on an emotional and spiritual one. Just as her body accompanied and reflected the intensity of her trauma with her defensive posture, illness and eating disorder, so too must her body be involved in the work so that it could assimilate the intensity of her healing. The act of kneeling, admittedly a moment of hyperbole, created an effect that escorted her into a space with men that she had never allowed herself to enter; one of giving respect and honor and asking for support. It was a holy moment.

To reinforce Marisa's new union and connection with men, I asked the men to interlock their arms and hands to form a human cradle for her. They gently lifted her and rocked her to a heartfelt song about needing and receiving. The whole group moved in around them; the sacredness of the moment was palpable—a transformation had taken place, and everyone felt it. It is difficult to describe the depth of joy and satisfaction I felt at this moment. My breath deepened and a wave of relief washed over me. I knew how critically important this achievement was for Marisa, and how it would significantly impact her well-being and future relationships.

"I definitely felt a shift both emotionally and physically. I used to be able to put up a good front that I was very strong. I could act like it, and physically was, but inside I was feeling really powerless, especially around relationships. I didn't really know what I wanted.

"Now, I'm in a place of power knowing what I want and what I want to create. I'm improving and opening my contact with people, especially men. And I can see changes in the choices that I make. I was in an unhealthy relationship with a man, which dragged on for a long time, about 10 years. We'd break up and then get back together. It was really hard and it was a very difficult decision to end

it, but it was one of the best choices I ever made. Three weeks later, at a wedding, I met my husband. He is the complete opposite of this other guy. He's supportive, reliable, and strong. All the work with Mariah has allowed me to be open to this kind of relationship. I moved through the really hard times and it's great because the work that I've done is now paying off.

"The other thing that opened up for me, along with owning my anger and feelings, was discovering a lot of creativity. I think this happened as a result of shedding most of the excess baggage I'd been carrying for so many years. I felt lighter and more open to other experiences and opportunities.

"Six years ago, I made a dream of mine become reality. I created a non-profit organization dedicated to offering safe, supportive and therapeutic services to children. It was a really wonderful thing to have that dream and then accomplish it."

Revealing and Healing Abuse

If you've experienced sexual, physical or emotional abuse, it is of paramount importance that you face that history head on, and discover the impact it has had for your behavior and relationships. In my more than 35 years as a psychotherapist, I have heard accounts of moments that have damaged people's lives that are so shocking and gruesome, that it hurts me to hear them: moments of cruelty, violence, horrific neglect, and physical and emotional abuse. I find myself saying, "No, that couldn't have happened. No one could or should ever go through something like this."

Whenever children are sexually abused, everything good they have ever believed about people and the world is ripped to shreds. Their innocence is stolen, along with their trust, self-esteem and sense of safety in the world. Unfortunately, many, if not most, blame themselves. They harbor the secret, initiating a pattern of isolation and self-destruction that can last a lifetime if they don't get help.

I have seen people whose entire lives were impacted by a single incident of childhood sexual abuse. I've also worked with victims of extreme sexual abuse with stories so shocking and disturbing that I find it hard to imagine how they ever survived it. All suffer.

If you were a victim of sexual abuse, what protective measures have you taken to survive? Do you retreat into addiction or isolation? Do you feel like damaged goods, unworthy of love and respect? Are you unable to imagine being loved by a healthy person? Do you mistrust people and life itself? Do you deny the damaging effects of your sexual abuse?

Every week in my office, I see victims of abuse who have been living lives of chaos and underdevelopment, often hiding addictions and distancing themselves from friends and family. They can be filled with pangs of intense emotions, including fear, anger and sorrow. Or they can present as numb and half-dead, devoid of any feelings. Their self-esteem is severely damaged and they are critical and blaming of themselves or others. They hide the truth, terrified of being authentic. Often they run from intimacy, not knowing how to deliver or receive love.

I know a woman who reported that her father came to her bedroom when he was drunk and molested her. She excused him telling herself it didn't really count because he was drunk and didn't know what he was doing. Meanwhile, she was obese and alcoholic. As a young woman, she had a period of promiscuity followed by a total distaste for and discomfort with anything sexual. Her denial of the damage kept her symptoms in place. Without even being aware of it, she was totally stuck in her reaction to the abuse.

If you were sexually, physically or emotionally abused, you need and deserve help. Keeping secrets not only prolongs your suffering but also delays your healing. Initiate a campaign of healing by telling someone you trust about your abuse. Then find excellent professional help in your hometown, or if necessary, travel to find the help you need. There are many excellent books on the subject of abuse and many qualified therapists to help you. My goal in these pages is to encourage and prepare you to begin your journey. I bear witness to the fact that people can and do heal all the time. If I could reach my hand out of this page to offer you support and encouragement to begin your healing journey, I would do it.

I'd like you to get a journal, and write down the abusive

moments you remember. Then see if you can identify unmet needs and unfinished business that are still alive in you. This list will be your configuration of needs and will include any moments of healing you know you need or would love to have. Understand and hear the needs of your deepest self. What do you need that would respond to and provide for the moments that still hurt you? As you have read, Marisa needed many moments to deliver her outrage, to get justice, to face her defenses and to do the work to transform them into healthier behaviors. She needed to confront her abuser. She needed the support of her family behind her.

Your Configuration of Needs

Your configuration of needs might seem extensive or impossible to meet. That's normal. You might need to release your outrage in a safe place or you might want an experience of cleansing. You might need to feel rescued and protected, experience the arms of a safe nurturing mother and/or father, or open up about your abuse to your spouse and friends. You might need justice, help improving your self-esteem or evidence of a world that is safe for you. You might need to experience the support of people who care about you or to meet other survivors of abuse to know that healing can happen. Your configuration of needs is unique to you and will serve as a map and a guide for your healing journey. Bring it to a professional whose skill and emotional connection you trust. Remember Marisa's work and know that it is never too late to receive what you need.

...speaking words of wisdom,
let it be, let it be.

—Beatles

Chapter Twelve

ANNA—RESURRECTING FAMILY RELATIONSHIPS

Anna was dying of breast cancer and was desperate—not to cure the cancer ravaging her body, she was beyond that, but to heal the "brokenness" within her family. For more than 20 years, she and her husband had endured a lifeless marriage, and their three grown children, a son and two daughters, were emotionally scarred by their parents' unhappiness. Her dying request was to have her entire immediate family come together under the same roof, one last time, to try to heal. In fact, there was so much bad history separating them that they had not been together for years. Anna's best friend, Marion, asked me to intervene with a *family intensive*, a series of family sessions spread over 2 days. As a practicing Buddhist, Marion wanted to offer a gift to Anna. Her gift was a reflection of her spiritual belief that we must rectify problems created in this lifetime so that they are not repeated in the next. Anna was shocked that all members of her family agreed to attend the intensive at her home in southern California.

At the time of Marion's request, I was leading a workshop at Esalen Institute in northern California, and had been planning to return home to my own family in 2 days. I was just finishing my second workshop, and was very tired. However, I knew Anna from a previous workshop, and I had both a professional and a spiritual interest in her well-being. I believed this to be such a sacred request, that I followed my heart and agreed to fly to southern California to do the family intervention.

Anna was emaciated and exhausted; more bones than flesh. Yet, within her heart and spirit there lived a passionate desire to attend to all the present pain, divisiveness and unspoken truths among her immediate family members. Frankly, I couldn't even imagine how Anna would find the strength and energy to participate in a 2-day intensive. Yet she was absolutely determined.

It is not an easy thing for family members to talk about their relationships with one another. Certainly, this family had never openly communicated their truths to one another. Instead, they had acted out their feelings by distancing and refusing to engage with each other. They were split into five isolated pieces. It was a tall order for me and for each of them to transform this family constellation within 2 days. However, the specter of death brings with it a transformational potential that can help people rise to their best selves. It is literally the last chance to get it right.

On the first day, everyone met at Marion's home where Anna had been living so that Marion could care for her. Marion's beautiful Spanish style home, with a red tile roof, sat on a hill overlooking mountains on one side and the ocean on the other. Tibetan flags hung along the patio wall.

Anna's husband, a handsome, impeccably dressed Italian man, was struggling to make juice both for Anna and me. Fresh vegetable juice for me, and wheatgrass juice, a powerful antioxidant with chlorophyll, for Anna. I felt sad for her that I wasn't spending the full 2 days on her marriage.

Anna's weak and emaciated body was propped up with pillows on the couch in the family room. Her skin barely covered her bones. Her hair, black a year ago, was now gray. The whites of her eyes were the color of butter. She was grateful I was there, yet frightened that this event might not succeed.

As she watched her husband and children enter the room, her eyes filled with tears. For her, this day was a dream come true. Her family did not share her joy. This was a deeply feeling, yet constricted, Italian American family who were obviously very uncomfortable with one another. They were unaccustomed to and somewhat skeptical of psychotherapy or any direct emotional exchange.

Johanna, a teenager and the youngest daughter, felt the closest to her mother; her impending loss was unbearable. When we were introduced, I sensed her depression and could see it in her body. Her chest was concave. As she walked with her feet close together, she lowered her head. Her shallow breath sputtered out in whispers. I learned later that the trauma of growing up in a family so devoid of love and honest communication had caused her to suffer a series of emotionally-related illnesses. She had chronic irritable bowel syndrome, was 20 pounds underweight, and had dropped out of school.

Her twenty-something sister, Karen, was distant, rigid, unexpressive and obviously angry. She was, however, well groomed and attractive. Her brother, Mark, macho, defensive and unemotional, stood with his arms crossed over his barrel-chest.

I could feel their tension in every fiber of my body and I had to work to relax as I made contact with this palpably pained family. Clearly, they weren't happy to be here or to meet me.

With so little time available, I started immediately by thanking each of them for coming and by acknowledging their courage. Under normal circumstances, it would take months to work with this family, but I had only 2 days. It was literally now or never. For Anna, the time constraint was even more pressing. At this point, only a miracle could reverse her grim prognosis.

As you have seen, music is an integral part of my work. I play music that matches the feeling or concern of each client at a particular moment. I selected carefully for this occasion and chose "The Living Years" by Mike and the Mechanics. The words of the song express the importance of saying what you have to say, your truth, while your family member is still alive.

When I asked the family to join hands and form a circle, they reluctantly reached out to one another. With a knot in my own stomach, I turned on the music, took a deep breath and prayed for assistance.

The music softened the tension in the room, and I began to sense an opening in this family's hard exterior. I coaxed them to go beyond their comfort zones while they looked directly into each other's eyes. I doubt if they had ever done that. The impact visibly moved them, some tears came, and the tension in their bodies released. As they each looked into Anna's eyes, their faces reflected the deep pain they all felt about the impending loss of their mother and wife.

Johanna began to sob with deep gasping breaths. I put my arms around her and helped her walk over to her mother. She dropped to her knees, took her mother's hands in hers and then put her head gently on her mother's chest, crying from the depths of her being.

Anna put her arms around her daughter. I was moved to tears, knowing this young girl was not ready to lose her mother. I know of my own struggle to stay alive for my sons until they no longer need me as an active parent. And I felt Anna's pain of knowing her children's growing years were far from successfully completed.

The other family members watched, noticeably moved by this outpouring of grief. They all had tears in their eyes. Even the gruff-looking brother wiped his eyes with a fisted hand.

When the music ended, I asked everyone to sit in a circle facing Anna. I then asked Anna to explain why this experience was important to her. Summoning as much strength as possible in her condition, she spoke from her heart saying she wanted a healing for the family before she died. She said she knew they were all in pain and had problems that came from unfinished business and unhealed hurts in the family. She could not die in peace unless they addressed the truth.

Then, after I asked her to address her children and her husband individually, Anna expressed her concerns, hopes, appreciation and love for each of them. One by one, they approached, and sat on a small stool next to the couch and faced her. She mentioned specific issues that she wanted to discuss and heal so that they could come together once again as a loving family. It took well over an hour for each. She went through how they were as children, what she knew about them; their strengths, weaknesses and vulnerabilities and worried that these characteristics might negatively affect their lives. She told each child what she wished for him or her and gave each the opportunity to tell her anything they needed to say or what they needed to hear.

Anna told her son how out of touch he was with his emotions and how this would interfere with his fulfillment in life should he fail to grow beyond his inhibitions. She expressed fear that her daughter's many stress-related illnesses eventually would develop into a serious disease and how she wanted her to learn how to care for herself.

Anna told her husband they should have divorced years ago because they were not compatible; they simply were too different as marriage partners. She needed a more spiritual and emotional relationship while he needed someone more traditional and Catholic, a wife who preferred home and hearth. When I heard her say that, I cringed, afraid it might distance him further (she recently had chosen to leave home and live with Marion). Her straightforwardness, however, elicited the opposite reaction in him. By sharing this unexpressed truth, they actually got in touch with their deep affection and respect for one another. As their hearts opened, they sobbed in one another's arms. From that moment, Anna's husband resumed his responsibility as her caregiver and even drove her to Mexico the following week to receive an experimental cancer treatment.

The children were all sobbing as the unspeakable was finally being spoken between husband and wife. They were letting out all the pain, built up over all those years, and relieved that it was out in the open and being talked about; they no longer had to pretend. Truth. The blessedness of truth.

Over the next 2 days, this family experienced complete openness for the first time in their lives. In a safe, loving, therapeutic environment, they were able to face many difficult and long-ignored painful issues.

At the end of this intensive work, feelings of gratitude and respect permeated the room. Together, we had made a life-altering journey that changed each of us for the better. I was relieved that it had gone so well and was filled with appreciation for the family's trust in me and for the courage displayed by this family.

Unfortunately, Anna's cancer did not go into remission. A short time later, she died peacefully with her husband and children lovingly by her side.

Anna's story is a powerful example of the miraculous potential of opening our hearts and minds to the healing of deep traumas or relationships. It is a story about the courage it takes to change and about the importance of a safe, loving environment in which to heal. It is about forgiveness and opening emotionally and expressing the truth to those you love. It is about the power of unfinished business and the significant role it plays in our lives.

Clearing Unfinished Business

None of us ever knows when death will take us by the hand and say: "It's your time now." Some of us, like Anna, are blessed with a warning and have a prolonged dying time before we take our final breath. We have spoken in another chapter about the importance of making peace with your relationship with death so that when your time comes, it will be less traumatic and you can approach it with creativity and emotional generosity to those you are leaving behind.

It had taken great courage for Anna to ask her family to do a family circle intensive that would involve examining the pain and needs of each person. It is not unusual for people to live for years with unspoken conflicts with friends and family, dooming the relationships to stagnation. This is an example of what can happen when a family pushes obvious problems under the rug in order not to voice the truth and face imagined consequences. In Anna's family, each member had taken on an isolated role in their pain and hurt and was trapped in silence and avoidance. Such a request requires family members to talk openly and authentically, perhaps for the first time in their lives, while bringing unfinished issues into the light and addressing them in skillful and mutually compassionate ways. In short, a family healing was achieved by managing old conflicts in new and effective ways, which is the art of completing unfinished business.

Anna underestimated the power of making a final request. Think about it. When you are in the dying process, you have enormous power to transform your life and heal your relationships. The fact is, it's hard for friends and relatives to deny a dying person's final request. Nor do they want to. It is also an opportunity to address unfinished business, which often takes the form of unexpressed resentments and/or unexpressed appreciations.

In the dying process, there is always the one dying and the ones remaining behind. Completion of unfinished business and sharing of present-day grief can be initiated by either the dying person or the ones left behind. When someone important to you is dying, figure out if there's anything you want or need to say to or hear from that person and make your request.

If a parent is dying, you may want to ask your whole family to pray together or engage in authentic dialogue. It is a time in families when petty issues can drop away and more meaningful issues can come to the surface for examination and healing. The most difficult death to mourn is one where active wounds remain. To carry sorrow about the loss of a loved one is tough enough; it is a much harder and more painful thing to carry anguish about unresolved issues with the deceased. The lack of healing is what lingers and can haunt you.

Think of the relationships you have experienced in your life.

How much unfinished business was left behind? Did you have or take the opportunity to speak your whole truth in a loving way? How about hearing from the other person? Did you hear what you needed to hear? Or are you left with an "if only" or "I should have," "I wish I could say" or "I wish I could hear"?

When you or a loved one is dying, how can you attend to unfinished business in a way that will bring understanding and closure? This is not a time to fight. The dying time is the time during which you need to be very creative and authentic. It's a time for being vulnerable, for asking for what you need, for skillfully reviewing and healing old hurts. Make apologies. Offer forgiveness. Express all your love and appreciation. Be bold, and go right to the heart of the matter:

"I'm sorry I took my anger out on you."

"I know we've been at odds for years, and I'm sorry for that."

"I need to hear you say you love me."

"Can you please forgive me?"

"I never told you enough how much you have given me, and how grateful I am."

"I wish I had done more to bring peace between us. Can we create that now?"

"I wish I had spent more time with you."

The transformation of Anna's fractured family into a loving one in 2 days is a testament to the power of clearing up unfinished business.

Being Alive and Whole

For me there is only the traveling on paths that have heart, on any path that may have heart. There I travel, and the only worthwhile challenge is to traverse its full length. And there I travel looking, looking, breathlessly.

—Don Juan, A Yacqui Sorcerer

Chapter Thirteen

BEING ALIVE AND WHOLE

Creating exact moments of healing is a simple, yet profound, formula. The knowledge of how to live fruitfully and how to mend emotional damage is so important that it should not be reserved exclusively for professionals. It needs to be disseminated into the general population. It is vital for all of us to develop the "know how" for creating and maintaining productive and harmonious relationships in our families, our communities and the world.

With this goal in mind, I designed this book as a tool to increase personal awareness, teach the mechanics of healthy contact, and reinforce the human capacity for bringing about change through the vitality of a loving heart.

It is critical to have the skills required to face and heal early wounds because it is these injuries that initiate the agenda for a lifetime of emotional development. We each have our own agendas and themes, and these themes will, in a sense, both follow us and guide us to our highest emotional potential in this lifetime. Or, if left unattended, these agendas can destroy our entire lives.

Equally important is the ability to know, respect and meet the continual emergence of your present needs and wants, the cycle of organismic self-regulation. Let it serve as your compass to find your center, your way home.

Along this path, you may find within you a configuration of unmet needs calling for provisions. Creating exact moments of healing offers a perfect response to these needs. To get there, you need to develop a keen sense of personal awareness as well as effective contact skills. Mature people have high levels of personal awareness and inhabit their whole being: body, mind, heart and soul. They are connected and have a rich inner life. They are clear about what they are experiencing now and about the messages their bodies are sending them. They have a healthy respect for the needs of their organism and a reverence in their relationship with themselves and others. They are *contactful* too. Developed people are ripe, juicy, colorful and clear in their interactions with others. They have an evolved capacity to make creative adjustments in difficult life circumstances. They design brilliant responses to their needs, express what they are feeling and move out on their own behalf.

It is your responsibility to get aligned with your needs by awakening into awareness and maximizing your capacity to love, provide and receive. This harmonious evolution of your whole being will gracefully unfold throughout your life and until you release your last breath.

This book has shown you that when you bring to your needs respect, love, compassion and generosity of spirit, you gain the capacity to transform your life, and contribute to the healing of others. In short, human need lies at the heart of potential change. It is the seed waiting for water.

In these pages, you also have read true stories of some of the hundreds of people who have changed their lives through this profound work and have seen the seminal moments that shaped their transformation. To them, I express my heartfelt gratitude.

These exact moments of healing addressed the transformative power of a loving relationship with one's body, the importance of receptivity in healthy human functioning, the need for supportive community, the empowerment manifested in fulfilling life's dreams, the development of a compassionate relationship with yourself and others, and recovery from sexual abuse and trauma.

I encourage you to live with transparency, knowing you are safer revealing your truth than you are covering it up with layers of armor. Feel the full range of your feelings. Create those moments of healing that soothe the cries of your soul and propel you forward in your personal evolution. Risk creating and fully entering those moments of vulnerability that will break your heart wide open and stretch your capacity to love.

A natural outgrowth of expanding your love and providing yourself with a successful healing journey will be the natural desire to spread your inner wealth. To that end, notice, inquire and care about the needs of others. If you are able, supply them with a moment of healing. Be curious about the moments of healing your loved ones need. Know them well; participate in their healing journeys. Create little sweet moments with strangers. Practice compassion for those you do not understand and forgiveness for the unforgivable. Pray for the healing of all people. Travel on the river that flows through the lives of everyone.

My hope is that the sharing of these stories, and tools for transformation, will have a ripple effect in a world so deeply in need of healing. I have a grand design, partly because life has taught me to think big. Thinking big includes never underestimating the power of one healthy human being. Remember, I've lived decades past the expiration date I was assigned, and I have personally attended transformations by the thousands, many of them long-shots. So I know better than to think small or to underestimate possibilities.

And here's what I think. The more people in the world providing exact moments of healing—whether spontaneously or with thoughtful intention—the more we will create peace in our hearts, our families, our community, our country, our world. Each of us is a powerful agent of change, and it is that power I hope to leave with each of you.

Changing the Past: A Gestalt Perspective on Trauma and Healing

Afterword

CHANGING THE PAST: A GESTALT PERSPECTIVE ON
TRAUMA AND HEALING — GORDON WHEELER

What is trauma? Why is it that some events, some experiences prove difficult or impossible to integrate into our living selves, while others, apparently just as severe or worse, seem to be assimilated organically into a person's core being, deeply heated or even transformed into strengths? Indeed, at times it seems that old wounds and stresses, even ones that would seem almost certainly overwhelming, have been so completely absorbed and assimilated into the living self that they become the very heart of a person's resources and capacities for empathy and creativity. In this important book, Mariah Fenton Gladis talks about this transformative healing in her own life and how she works with others to approach the same depth and freedom for themselves, plainly drawing on her own wounds and her own healing to co-create this magical work. How do transformations like that happen—and for that matter what is it that keeps them from happening all the time in our patients and clients, our loved ones and in our own lives? What are the necessary conditions of healing that make for that alchemy that transforms injury into inspiration, stress into resilience and traumatic losses and life events into the gold of a creative and compassionate heart?

Everything that doesn't kill you helps you grow, my old grandmother was fond of saying, with a sort of determined shrug. Alas, we know things are not always so simple. However much value that affirmation may have as a reminder of our innate potential for survival and renewal, the truth is that all of us know people who are living—or is it just surviving?—with only a limited part of themselves available for new experience, new creative energy and growth. Meanwhile other parts, sometimes the greater parts, remain mired in an old matrix of hurt and shame, fear and rage and an uncanny tendency to encounter again, in ever new situations and relationships, the very injuries and frustrations that remain undigested and unhealed from a difficult past. And if we are really honest, isn't something like this true for all or nearly all of us, with some issues or relationships at least? In more parts of our lives than we'd like to admit?

How should we think about painful issues and dynamics like these? Whether we speak of transference, maladaptive schemes, repetition compulsion, family induction, unfinished business, or the explanatory terms and concepts of any other model, several things seem always to characterize stuck and destructive patterns of this kind. First of all, they don't just go away by themselves. To be sure, some habits do fade or change easily—provided that they are no more than habits, ordinary learned patterns not held in place by strong feeling and then reinforced dynamically each time we go through them.

Deep wounds and trauma, on the other hand, have more the dynamic structure of phobias, which are self-reinforcing by nature. That is, each time we encounter a phobic or traumatic situation, the rigid or ritualized reaction patterns we learned long ago that serve to get us over or away from the experience somehow, and the reduction of anxiety we then feel, only serve to reinforce the dysfunctional reactive pattern itself. Thus, our worst fears and most rigid reactions may only solidify and grow over the years, even without any renewed trauma—however self-defeating or paralyzing or even bizarre those reactions may look to the outside observer or even to us. In this way, a self-destructive behavior or habit may come to take on the dynamic character of an addiction. We adopt rigid behavioral patterns to help us deal with more affect, more emotions that are too intense to support than we know how to support without recourse to some familiar, addictive dulling or soothing action. Thus addictions too are self-reinforcing and may grow stronger even as they undermine other, healthier adaptations and behaviors in other parts of our lives. Many of these rigid patterns are of course fairly benign, but others—drinking, drugging, compulsive gambling or sexuality, violence toward self or others, and so on—are terribly destructive and terribly resistant to change as we know, for all the very reasons we've just been outlining here.

The second thing about deep pain and trauma of this kind is the way we tend to return to these experiences again and again to seek them out and reenact them in an eerie and often destructive repetition. If the feelings and the reactions—oftentimes knee-jerk stereotyped reactions we go through every time we're faced with anything that reminds us of the old traumatic events or relationships—don't go away by themselves, neither do the occasions for encountering them again, with maddening or depressing regularity. If my parent was harsh and abusively critical, then I may find my voice is paralyzed (or I fly into a rage) every time I encounter any criticism, and yet I am strangely drawn to people with that same defensive pattern, often making them my adversaries, my intimate partners, or both.

How we account for this kind of recurrence depends entirely on how we view human nature, and the nature and characteristics of the living self. If we see people as isolated individual sources of libidinal/aggressive charge in search of release and understand life as a process of tension reduction in the way characterized by a certain strain of Freud's thinking, then we will begin to think in terms of cathexis and canalization of energy, the search for the familiar (punitive, depriving) object, masochism and the repetition compulsion. If we think of people as, say, Skinner did, as "black boxes" responding directly to reinforcement contingencies, then we will assume maladaptive learning. If we are primarily sub elements of a family system, then we will think in terms of role and delegation, individuation and distress within the parental couple. In each case our interventions as we try to help people who are locked in these old patterns will differ and will follow from what we understand to be the nature of the problem and of people themselves.

Mariah Fenton Gladis works out of the terms and premises of the Gestalt model, which rests on the core insight that our experience and behavior are a unified, active construction of and on the whole field of our experience. This construction consists of the "Inner World" of our own memories, feelings, beliefs, fears and longings and dreams, together with our understanding of the "Outer World" of resources and conditions, dangers and supports, conditions known and unknown, and above all, other people, who may be all of these things to us and more. Thus, the Gestalt perspective sees people as active, creative problem-solvers, constructing and then dealing as best we can with a field of experience, in the service of our natural need to survive, thrive, and grow. The "one drive" of human nature, as Gestalt neurologist Kurt Goldstein argued in 1940, is the "drive to organize experience," to construct meaningful, workable wholes (or "schemas" as they are called in current cognitive models, much based on Goldstein's work) because it is these organized wholes of understanding and action that enable us to solve problems in living and managing our worlds and our lives. Thus Gestalt takes its place, fundamentally, as evolutionary psychology; we are "wired for meaning" because meaning enables us to estimate and predict, which are in turn the essential elements of our remarkable problem-solving capacities, as a small and individually helpless species in a difficult and often shifting world. Human beings, after all, are the animals that aren't good at much of anything, except just that: getting together and doing creative problem solving.

Our behavior, in other words, is never just a simple matter of reaction and reinforcement, or learning contingencies and training. We aren't driven by event, by "what happens to us," but by the meaning of it we construct, now and in the past, the context we understand an event to be a part of, which shapes how we will hold that memory and what solutions to it may then strike us as possible, impossible or simply unthinkable in the first place. This is why humans are also the species prone to neurosis and what we call "mental illness." Because of the way we live, always and necessarily, so much in our creative imaginations, the rich, active ferment of that creative problem-solving capacity is the very essence of the living self in action. Where instinct is low, social learning will be high, and where relational bonding and interactive learning are high, the potential for mislearning and maladaptation will be correspondingly high as well. Change those, that imagination and memory, and the context of feeling and value around them, and you will change the behavior as well. Or to say the same thing the other way around, if you want to open up a person's reactions and behavior to a new repertory of creative possibilities, you have to change the experiential meaning, the fabric of belief and memory and body sensations and feelings themselves that are holding those old patterns in place and blocking or clouding the view to anything new. This understanding and these creative assumptions lie at the heart of Mariah's work.

This leads us to the next characteristic of the traumatic stress and event, which has to do with the context and conditions of painful and powerfully stuck dynamics like these in our lives; experience that is undergone alone and is held now in too alone a way.

Next, construction of emblematic scenes—the way we encapsulate and codify memory (bad and good) in such scenes. It doesn't matter if the scene we remember is literally exactly how it happened. It is how we are carrying it now. Memory, like all of our experience in the Gestalt view, is a construction, not a videotape.

In other words, memory is a narrative—a meaningful series or sequence—"stored" as a whole sequence: this leads to that leads to that, given such and such conditions. This has to be true because the evolutionary point of awareness is for prediction: It is constructing our worlds into "narrative" that makes experience manageable; experience is always organized, in this sense.

What is therapy? The deconstruction of experience and the study, together with one or more other people, of how I construct my world. Therapy is done with another person because that construction was my understanding, which I constructed to manage the world, in other words, to manage anxiety, helplessness and shame. If I deconstruct that picture now, for example, that all women are depriving, that all strong people are going to leave me no space, that all sexuality is predatory, that all intimacy is dangerous and so on, the anxiety and shame that were "solved" by that old view, those old behaviors, will initially come flooding back. I need someone there, that extra support, so that the aloneness with those feelings that I felt back then isn't just recapitulated and reinforced. Alone means shame and, in the end, trauma cannot be healed alone. Healing always takes place in relational context. This goes to the definition of trauma and follows from everything I've said.

Given this much, we can say what the criteria and conditions of an individual's transformational healing must be: the deconstruction of their old story and the construction of a new narrative in the context of others who are truly interested. The form of healing work created and offered here by Mariah fits these criteria.

Can a moment do it? Yes and no. Unblocking. Mariah writes of the unblocking effect of the new memory paired with the old. The effect is *destructuring*. At times we can make a dramatic shift, which opens up a new possibility in the field. Such shifts can be transformative, not because they are "one-trial learning" but because of their lasting deconstructive effects. Mariah writes of this when she describes pairing the new memory, the new outcome experience, with the old. If both are present, a productive tension, an energized space is created, and in that energized space, life itself becomes a creative experiment.

All dedicated teachers have something they care about imparting; all try at least to talk the talk. Truly inspiring teachers also walk the walk; they embody, in their own lives and work, the principals they teach, and at this point teaching becomes healing. Mariah Fenton Gladis is an inspiring teacher and healer in this sense: her gift and her message begins with her own presence. Remarkably, that gift and that presence comes right through on the page and touches us intimately, profoundly. To the fortunate reader, this book is an inspiring deconstruction of some of your own ideas, a transformational learning experience, and a personal treat. Enjoy!

Gordon Wheeler, PhD
President
Esalen Institute
Big Sur, California

Tales of a Wounded Healer

Appendix

JACK'S LETTER TO ME

Dear Mariah,

I want to thank you for the encouragement and healing that you gave to me when I attended your weekend workshop at the Pennsylvania Gestalt Center this past June. The experience was so powerful and has provided me with rewards far beyond anything that I had ever expected.

You may remember, after my open seat work, you recommended that I try to find my mother to see if I could reconcile with her. I was not immediately receptive to your suggestion, but after returning home and talking to Gail (my wife), I decided to begin a search for her. I also decided to reconnect with relatives from whom I had (through my own actions) become separated.

I made a "pilgrimage" back to my childhood home in Maryland the first weekend in August. There were two intentions to my visit: (1) to reconnect with aunts, uncles, and cousins whom I hadn't seen since my dad died over 22 years ago, and (2) to go to the house where my mother lived when I last saw her in January 1974. I captured my experiences and impressions of that trip in a journal, and I have included a copy of it with this letter. Please feel free to share it with your colleagues and other members of the Pennsylvania Gestalt Center, as you feel appropriate.

Subsequent to the events described in my journal, I wrote my mother a letter, and sent her a copy of my journal, along with numerous pictures of me throughout my life. Then my mother called, and we had a very emotional crying and laughing conversation, ending with her saying that she wanted to come up to Connecticut to meet me!!! We settled on a date—the weekend of September 13-14. As you can no doubt imagine, I was overjoyed, scared, anxious, excited, hesitant, exhilarated. I felt like a little boy again waiting for Christmas.

Well, my mother came to visit this past weekend and it was a fantastic success. We laughed, cried, and told stories—we exchanged hurts and dreams. Most of all, I got to hear my mom's side of the story of our separation. As I suspected, my dad and grandma hadn't told the whole truth. I told her about my experience at your workshop—how (in the role-play) you had my grandma encourage me to go with my mom and how she (my mom) welcomed me into her arms and embraced me and told me that she loved me and would never leave me again. She shared some of the things that she dealt with through her own therapy sessions. Needless to say, the reunion was really powerful for both of us. When we parted, she hugged me and said, "I have three sons!"

There's obviously a lot more to tell. But I won't go into any more details now. I may write more in my journal and if I do, I will send that to you.

One of the things that this has done is to help me bring closure, because she and I have been able to talk about why she left my father, and why she never followed up with letters to me. She said that's one of the things she felt the most regretful for. She had opportunity then, and she was afraid to do anything about it.

I do sincerely thank you from the depths of my heart for helping me to achieve this healing. Your clarity of perception, gentle energy, and sincerity of spirit kindled in me the courage to reach out to my mom. My mom and I were able to come together with open hearts and arms, each exposing our vulnerabilities to the other and each having the reward of unconditional love extended in return. I felt no anger toward her. And we never let remorse for so much time lost creep in to interfere.

I feel blessed to have had such a powerfully positive and loving experience at your workshop. And then, to leave and have the role-play actually be played out in real life is just so incredibly magical. I will hold you in my heart always for how your wisdom and loving kindness have helped me.

With Love,

Jack

Jack's Mother's Letter

August 9, 1996

Dear Jack,

I received a letter from a former neighbor explaining that you and your wife were there about a week ago looking for me. We weren't home when she called, and our answering machine has been acting up lately. Please don't be too angry with her; she simply didn't want to give any information out without first conferring with me. I would have done the same.

I guess you're wondering how I found your home address. Ed (your stepbrother) is a policeman in Alabama. I asked him to help to locate you—giving him your place of work, full name, date of birth, WI, MD, NY, CT. I had found you through the "88 million households" software program. I had looked through WI and MD right after we got the computer but found nothing. Besides, it was an older program.

I have thought of you so often—wondering where you were, what you were doing, how things were in your life. Maybe now we can forge a relationship. I'm not asking for anything spectacular— too much time has passed—but something that we can both be comfortable with. This is the reason that I'm writing instead of calling. It will give you time to think over what I am writing and then, perhaps, make the next move.

"Nanny," your great grandmother, died in June '94 after several years of coping with congestive heart disease. She was almost 92 years old. She was completely worn out physically during the last few months.

Dean, your other stepbrother, lives in St George, WV. He is currently working at a lumber mill and has a wife and one son. Ed is in Hueytown, AL and married. He also has three children by previous marriages.

We officially moved to Winchester, VA in Fall '91 after 10 years of living in two states and building on our own. It has been a tremendous amount of work but worth it. We are still making changes and adding little touches to the outside—each Spring I think of a new project for Don to do!

This letter will give you a thumbnail sketch of the past few years. Please write or call. I'm not on-line, so there's no e-mail address. Perhaps in the near future, we can meet and find out where to go from here. I would like that very much.

Love,

Your Mother (signed)

CPSIA information can be obtained at www.ICGtesting.com
Printed in the USA
BVOW081536200513

321170BV00001B/1/P